STANDOUT OR DIE

How to make your DIGITAL MARKETING AGENCY more visible, desirable and valuable

GARETH HEALEY

Published by Goldcrest Books International Ltd
www.goldcrestbooks.com
publish@goldcrestbooks.com

ISBN: 978-1-913719-40-1
eISBN:978-1-913719-41-8

For Emma and Callum

My **STANDOUT** *achievements.*

CONTENTS

FOREWORD

I have been supporting, advising, and benchmarking agencies since 2004. It all started with The Wow Company, an accounting practice I co-founded that specialises in working with agencies. Seeing the accounts of these agencies made me curious. Why was it that some agencies grew quickly and profitably, whilst others got stuck, or went out of business?

I wanted to find out more, so I started benchmarking agencies, sharing statistics, trends and insights from the top-performing agencies each year in BenchPress – now the largest survey of independent agencies in the UK.

I also co-founded The Agency Collective – a wonderful community of agency owners that support each other through the challenges of running an agency. We have over 700 members around the world, and I learn so much from hearing their stories.

Throughout all of my time working with agencies, I've seen one consistent truth. The agencies that specialise in either a sector niche, or a technical specialism (or both), grow faster and make more profit than those that are generalist. But there's so much more to becoming a successful agency than simply focusing on a niche. That's why I was thrilled to see that Gareth had written this book.

Hearing from someone who's been there, seen it, and done it, is always useful. The lessons they've learned along the way provide valuable insights to help us on our own journey. However, Gareth has done much more than simply share his story in this book. He's provided a practical, step-by-step framework to guide you on the path to creating the agency you've always dreamed of.

Reading the story of Adrian and his agency, Treadmill, reminded me of so many conversations I've had with agency owners over the years. Gareth's description of Adrian beautifully captures the challenges and stresses of running an agency. If you've ever felt like you're stuck, working long hours without making much progress, this book gives you the opportunity to break that cycle.

I've seen so many examples over the years of agencies that have followed the principles that Gareth shares in this book and seen transformational results. One that stands out was a small creative agency I met in 2011. I nearly fell off my chair when they told me their hourly rate was only £40/hour – well below the average at the time. Back then, the agency was building websites for local businesses, charging £1,500 per time, working crazy hours for not much money. They knew they needed to change.

Over the coming months, they worked hard on their proposition and the type of clients that they wanted to work with. They focused on a niche (internal communications) and started to work with larger clients. Their hourly rate increased, slowly at first, and then much faster as they built their confidence. Two years on from that first conversation, they had repositioned themselves as experts in internal communications. They were winning £100,000 projects with blue-chip brands, charging based on value rather than time, with an average effective hourly rate of £150/hour. They decided to stand out from the crowd and have not looked back since.

This story is a wonderful example of what awaits if you're prepared to start your journey to being STANDOUT. This book will show you how to do it.

Thank you to Gareth for taking the time to write something so useful, practical, and powerful.

Peter Czapp

Co-Founder The Wow Company
and The Agency Collective.

INTRODUCTION

My Story

Twenty-five years ago I fell in love; not once, but twice. The first time was with a beautiful woman, who I am proud to say is now my wife. The second time was with a career.

After graduating from De Montfort University, I started a job as an account handler in a below-the-line marketing agency. I knew agency life was for me from the first day I walked through the door.

The term below-the-line has largely disappeared. It was used to describe an agency that used marketing channels and tactics other than paid media (TV, radio, press, etc.). Paid was the realm of the above-the-line advertising agencies.

My agency utilised direct mail, promotions, events and other owned channels. Our focus was on delivering fast, measurable results. In many ways, it was a precursor to the performance-focused nature of digital marketing.

After four years, and eager for broader experience, I moved to a design agency in Leeds to head up their biggest account. Less than two years later, the founder announced that he wanted to retire. He asked if I wanted to be part of a management buyout team. We completed the MBO in 2002.

For the next 15 years I led the business as Chief Executive Officer (CEO). We grew it into a £12.5 million, integrated creative agency, working with some of the biggest names in UK retail. We were acknowledged as the top regional agency in the UK and employed 175 staff across offices in Leeds and London. As well as many awards for our client work, we also were recognised for our investment in, and commitment to, our people and culture.

In 2017, I exited my agency. In search of a fresh challenge, I sold my 50% equity to my business partner. Finding agency life too difficult to leave behind completely, I founded a specialist consulting firm called Beyond Noise. I now work exclusively with ambitious, independent agency owners, training and coaching them to build more profitable, sustainable and enjoyable businesses. Whilst my career has pivoted, my passion for the agency sector has not diminished, in fact, it's found a new lease of life!

Why I wrote this book

I've always wanted to write a book. I started writing this one in March 2020. The UK, like much of the world, had gone into lockdown due to COVID-19. It was a terrible situation, but it seemed like the perfect opportunity to realise my dream of becoming a published author.

As a series of lockdowns came and went, my admiration for other authors skyrocketed. *STANDOUT OR DIE* took me far longer, and was much harder to write, than I ever imagined. It was a very steep learning curve for me, but if it helps you and your agency in some way, it will have been worth it.

Despite my desire to be an author, and the situation, this book isn't a product of circumstance. It was never just a way of avoiding too much Netflix during isolation. As we embarked upon a new decade, the pandemic wasn't the only thing on my mind. I was frustrated. The marketing agency sector – the sector I loved – was in a mess.

What was once an exciting and aspirational industry seemed to be losing its sparkle. Fewer people were seeing agencies as an attractive career choice. Even before the pandemic hit, many agency owners seemed disillusioned and demotivated.

It seemed as if agencies had all started to look, sound and act the same. The UK agency landscape had settled in an all too familiar pattern. At one end, the big networks and London-based firms continued to win the big clients. At the other end, an endless stream of freelancers and new start-up agencies battled for any clients they could find. Occupying the middle ground were thousands of mid-sized independents, many calling themselves 'digital agencies'.

Lots of these agencies were great businesses run by talented people. But many more were not going anywhere particularly fast. Their growth and ambition had long since plateaued. They seemed content to be making up the numbers and almost happy to blend in. I wondered what the economic impact of the pandemic was going to do to these agencies. Running an agency has always demanded immense stamina and resilience. Competing in the post-pandemic world will be harder than ever. They couldn't afford to stand still. They needed to take action. Some were even facing a battle for survival.

I came to the conclusion that the world didn't need *more* digital agencies – it needed *better* digital agencies. I wrote this book to help established agencies who were stalled to shift gears. I wanted to help those agencies who had lost their way, or those that were competing hard but still treading water. I resolved to write a book that would help them move from STANDSTILL agencies and become STANDOUT agencies.

If you run a digital agency, doing the same things as everybody else will no longer be enough. You can't afford to be an ordinary agency; you're going to need to be extraordinary. You must stand out from the crowd.

Part 2 of this book will introduce you to the seven principles I call the STANDOUT agency R.O.A.D.M.A.P. These tried-and-tested methods are designed to make your agency more visible, desirable and valuable.

If you want to attract and retain better clients, recruit loyal people and enjoy running and growing your agency into a valuable asset, this book will show you how.

Who is this book for?

As you'll discover later, defining a target audience is one of the most important factors in becoming a STANDOUT agency. Most STANDSTILL agencies fail to recognise this (or at least do anything about it).

In Chapter 2, you're going to meet Adrian, an avatar of my audience, but in summary this book is for ...

Owners-directors of digital agencies between £500,000 and £1 million of annual gross profit. They have more than 10 staff and have been trading for more than 3 years. They don't want to build the biggest agency in the world, but they do want to grow. Unfortunately, their growth has stalled. They're unhappy. They're struggling to win new business, recruit staff and stay motivated themselves.

Oh wait, that's not you? Stay with me. Don't go anywhere. At least finish reading this section (please).

My target audience is very specific. There's good reason for this. Despite my own background running a large integrated firm, I'm fascinated by digital agencies. There's plenty of them around but as a genre they must evolve. Since leaving my own business I've also realised I love working with smaller agencies. The people running them tend to be ambitious, keen to learn and able to make quick decisions. To get maximum value from working with me, they need to have earned their stripes though. They need to have been in business for a length of time and already learned from some of their own mistakes. And they need to be hungry. If the fire in their bellies has completely gone out, or was never really there in the first place, then I can't help them. I can fuel the fire, but only they can light it.

Here's the thing. If the above description doesn't EXACTLY describe you, that's OK. You can still get massive value from reading this book.

If you're remotely involved in marketing (NB: everybody in business is), you need a target audience. But you also need to understand that your target is not your market. Your target is the bullseye, your market is much wider. Many more people are able to get value from, or buy from you, than those that you specifically communicate with.

- **You're NOT running a digital agency.** Agency business models are the same. I started my career before digital marketing was a thing, so my own experience is not only digital. In my work with Beyond Noise I've worked with creative agencies, PR firms, Media agencies and software companies. I've applied the same principles and got the same positive results with all types of agencies.

- **You're a small agency, or even a freelancer just starting out.** You are at the start of your journey. As you will see later I passionately believe that's what running an agency is – a journey. With this book you can learn new things and arm yourself for the challenges to come. You can learn from my mistakes and avoid making them yourself.

- **You're running a large agency with 50 people or more**. Congratulations, that's a fantastic achievement. You didn't get there by not learning from others though. Like me, you will have also forgotten some great lessons along the way. I guarantee this book will teach you something new. It will also help you recall some things that you know but need a gentle reminder to refocus on.

- **You're running a sub £1 million agency and have been for many years.** On average, it takes UK agencies seven years to reach £1 million billings.[1] Billing over £1 million is a target for many smaller agency owners. As many as 83% say it is a target they want to achieve.[2] In reality £1 million billings

1. BenchPress 'Under £1M Report 2021'
2. BenchPress 'Agency Milestones'

is a goal and nothing more. For some people, not hitting it is a complete failure, for others, it's not even on their radar. If you've been running your agency longer than seven years you may not want it to hit £1 million revenue. Bigger might not be your goal, but if you've read this far you do want something. You want it to be better. This book can show you how.

- **You're NOT running an agency at all.** The principles in this book can be applied to many other types of businesses, particularly but not limited to, business services. If you run a legal firm, accountancy practice or HR consultancy, don't be put off by references to digital agencies. There's something here for you.

No one agency, or one agency owner, is the same. Some people are happy to coast along running their business. They're comfortable with the status quo. But I find most agency owners are more ambitious. Many are also frustrated. They're not satisfied with their progress or their role within the business. Their problem is they don't know what to do about it.

STANDOUT OR DIE outlines my key learnings from running my own agency for 15 years and my experiences from helping other agency owners to grow their businesses.

You have an opportunity to make your business into a STANDOUT agency. Let the STANDOUT agency R.O.A.D.M.A.P. guide you.

Gareth Healey
November 2021

PART 1

WHY STANDOUT?

CHAPTER 1

COMPETITION AND COMPLACENCY

Success can lead to complacency, and complacency is the greatest enemy of success.

Brian Tracy, author and speaker

Digital, or New-Media agencies as they were then called, first appeared in the late 1990s. They created early websites and tools such as CD-ROMs. Back then they were niche players. They were new, different and specialists in their field.

Today, digital agencies dominate. There are somewhere between 25,000 and 30,000 marketing agencies in the UK alone. A large proportion describe themselves as 'digital agencies'. Some specialise, most offer a range of services across many channels and platforms.

The reason digital agencies are such a success is obvious. Demand for digital marketing has exploded since the turn of the millennium. It even increased during the COVID-19 pandemic as more businesses moved their operations online.

Whilst high demand is a good thing, it can come at a price. Wherever you find high demand, you also find complacency. Suppliers in the market become too comfortable, sometimes even lazy. Standards and service levels can suffer. Innovation can be stifled.

Unfortunately, complacency is alive and well in the digital agency sector. There is a misplaced sense of security in some sections of the community. They operate in what is now a mature market, but digital agencies still seem to view themselves as being somehow new and different. They seem to believe that they'll continue to thrive no matter what the economic conditions. There's a perpetuating myth that digital agencies are easy to scale and sell. A belief that multi-million pound exits are common and easily achievable. The reality is quite different.

Operating a decent digital agency is not difficult. There are far harder ways of making a living. But there's a big difference between running a digital agency and running a great digital agency. That difference is about to become even more pronounced and important.

There's a saying that 'a rising tide lifts all boats'. Whilst demand remains high, we're entering a new phase of the agency market. The tide may not be going out, but the number of boats in the water is a growing problem. The market is becoming saturated. The skills and services agencies provide are becoming commoditised. It's hard to choose between different firms, or to even know where to start.

The fact is digital agencies are in danger. It's no longer good enough to be an ordinary agency. It's not OK to be just OK. Agencies are no different from any other business or sector. If they want to continue to survive and thrive they must evolve.

I don't subscribe to the thinking that the agency model is broken. But if you own a digital agency in the 2020s, you can't afford to be complacent. You're going to come under threat from more competition than ever before.

This book is your wake-up call, but it's also your salvation. You're going to need to change. You're going to need to stand out from the crowd. This book is going to show you how.

Demand and Supply

Demand is not the only reason why there are so many digital agencies. The barriers to entering the market are almost non-existent. Anybody can set up an agency. You don't need a licence, qualifications, or even previous experience. There's no mandatory training, regulation, standards, or even a code of ethics. This isn't a problem for those people that aren't experienced or qualified. It is a problem for those that are. It may well be a problem for you. How do you convince clients that you know what you're doing when so many other people are sending out the same message?

Agencies are not only easy but quick to start up. Unlike many businesses, they need very little capital investment. With a laptop and an internet connection, you can be the proud owner of a new agency in a couple of hours. It's not surprising then that so many people start them, or the quality is so variable.

With so few barriers, it's little wonder new start-ups continue to enter the market. Usually, more players means more competition. Oversupply in a market encourages price competition. In most sectors there are large, dominant businesses. They deter new entrants by undercutting them and making the market less attractive.

Whilst it's easy to start a digital agency, it's very difficult to scale one. If you can't sell to a large volume of customers, you can't scale. You can't take advantage of economies of scale (the cost advantages derived from size). It's these economies that lower prices. This doesn't happen in the agency world.

Whilst you can't avoid competition, nobody in the digital agency space wants to compete on price. It's not a sustainable business model. If you want to avoid the price trap, you're going to need to compete in other areas. The R.O.A.D.M.A.P. I'm going to introduce you to will be your guide.

Technology and Disruption

If competition from other firms wasn't enough, digital agencies are also under pressure from elsewhere. Technology companies and platforms create a demand for the skills that agencies provide. Agencies exist in the space between the technology, their clients, and their clients' customers. This is not a bad thing, but it means they're connectors or middlemen.

Technology is extremely effective at reducing and shortening supply chains. It cuts out middlemen. It's the secret sauce of most online businesses. Tech has made it easy for even inexperienced people to build websites, create content, or do their own advertising. Pre-digital, owners of traditional media didn't want to deal directly with brands or the general public. Media agencies managed these relationships and sold their advertising space for them. Today, the digital media platforms encourage a direct relationship with their end users.

Digital agencies now compete with many of the tools that they generate revenue from. A recent survey revealed that on average, CMOs (Chief Marketing Officers) currently allocate about a quarter of their budgets (23.7%) to agencies and their services. Spending on marketing technology now surpasses this at 26.2%.[3] New technology has benefited every industry on the planet. But it has also disrupted and even destroyed some. Could this be the fate of digital agencies?

The digital agency landscape is changing. Channels and platforms have proliferated. Google constantly changes its algorithms and has become more opaque. Privacy laws like General Data Protection Regulation (GDPR) and policy changes by the tech giants, are restricting how we're able to collect and use data. Tools like Facebook's campaign budget optimisation (CBO), and start-ups like www.copy.ai, are taking the effort, subjectivity, and even expertise, out of digital advertising creative and media placement.

The challenge facing digital agencies, therefore, is not just competition from their peers. It's the fact that they might be squeezed out altogether. As agencies can use technology, tools and media platforms, so too can their clients. The data collected by the tech giants gives them

---

3. www.gartner.com/en/marketing/research/annual-cmo-spend-survey-research

more insight into customer behaviour than agencies could ever dream of; firepower that is unmatchable even by the global agency networks.

These challenges are daunting, but if you own a digital agency, you don't have to compete with the tech giants to be successful. You do have to be better than the other agencies that compete against you. The principles I reveal later in this book will help you.

Trust and Loyalty

Whilst brands appear to be placing their trust in Marketing Technology (MarTech), trust in agencies is in rapid decline. Research conducted by CreativeRace in association with YouGov revealed an astonishing 34% of UK CMOs say they have little or no trust in agencies.[4]

There are signs that these views are reflected by the general public. A 2021 survey ranked Advertising Executives as the second least trusted people, just above social media influencers. Even politicians were considered to be more trustworthy![5]

It's unclear exactly what the reasons are behind this. Poor standards, quality control, opaque pricing, and a lack of appreciation of what agencies do must all contribute. Unfortunately, lack of trust breeds insecurity and that impacts client loyalty.

4. https://creativerace.co.uk/wp-content/uploads/2021/03/CMO-Whitepaper-Final.pdf
5. www.ipsos.com/sites/default/files/ct/news/documents/2021-03/veracity_index_2021_2.pdf

The bad news is that clients are switching agencies more than ever before. They're also less inclined to sign long-term contracts (if they sign contracts at all). Demand might be high but if your agency doesn't keep – as well as win – clients, you'll never build a sustainable business. The good news is that the principles in this book will help you establish something so many agencies don't have – trust and loyalty within a specific target market.

Speed and Data

Whether they trust agencies or not, clients are changing how they use them. An increasing number of larger brands have set up their own studios and digital marketing teams. In the past in-housing marketing services has always been cyclical. Many clients have built internal teams, only for their Financial Directors to challenge why they've created such a large, fixed overhead.

The current trend for in-housing is different though. In the past, the main advantage was brand and market knowledge. Today it's speed and data. Clients often need to make changes to their websites immediately. Social media channels are in real-time dialogue with customers and must be responsive. Brands want to analyse, interpret and protect their own data. It has far wider implications than the development of the next marketing campaign. A recent survey reported that almost 32% of work has shifted from external agencies to in-house teams.[6]

6. Gartner 2020 CMO Spend Survey https://emtemp.gcom.cloud/ngw/globalassets/en/marketing/documents/cmo-spend-survey-part2.pdf

Access and Alternatives

It's not just big clients that are changing how they work; smaller clients now have more options than ever at their disposal. Agencies are already in competition with the freelance community and platforms like Upwork Inc.™ that give access to them. The pandemic didn't start this trend, but it may fuel it further. Freelancing and the gig economy was increasing before the pandemic. The events of 2020 mean freelancing has become even more popular from both a supply and demand perspective. It's an alternative to both working for, and working with, an agency.

It's long been possible for clients to access digital skills across the globe. For cost conscious clients in the West, the lower cost of services provided by skilled people in countries like The Philippines, Indonesia and India may be even more attractive in the future.

The seven principles in this book, won't stop your clients from offshoring some of their work if they really want to. They will help them to choose your agency over others and give them fewer reasons to look elsewhere.

Adapt and Change

Agencies are not unique in operating in crowded and competitive environments. They're far from being the only industry threatened by new technology and changing buying habits. A competitive market requires its participants to differentiate. Creativity and innovation usually help some competitors rise above the rest.

Sadly, the herd mentality seems strong amongst agencies. There's a lack of variety or individualism. There is little differentiation in the sector, and barring a few of the bigger groups, limited brand awareness. Whilst there are more varieties of agencies than ever, there are also more people saying the same things, doing the same things and repeating the same mistakes.

The digital agency sector has been slow to change and adapt. Standing out in such a crowded market is extremely difficult, but it's never been more vital for agencies to do so. Marketing agencies have always been at the forefront of change. As marketers, our primary purpose and value is to spot, interpret and capitalise on new developments. We're great at doing this for our clients; we must now do the same for ourselves.

The future is never certain. What is clear though is that whilst we live in extraordinary times, there will be no place for ordinary agencies. Digital transformation will continue, demand and opportunities will remain, but so will the number of digital agencies ready to exploit them. If your business is not offering something different, tangible, and meaningful, you're going to blend into the background. If you want to build a successful digital agency, you'll need to stand out from the crowd.

The life of an agency owner is getting tougher. For some digital agency owners, it could be a battle for survival. For the rest, only those agencies that can stand out above the noise will thrive. If there was ever an opportunity for taking stock, re-evaluating and deciding to do things differently, now is that time. Standing out has never been more critical. You may even have to standout or die!

CHAPTER 2

STANDSTILL AGENCIES

It is not the strongest of the species that survives, nor the most intelligent. It is the one that is the most adaptable to change.

Charles Darwin

In the previous chapter we looked at the dynamics that are shaping the digital agency sector. We now know the major causes of an agency owner's problems. But what are the symptoms? What are the daily headaches that plague them? What issues do they have? What mistakes do they make?

To help us explore these challenges, I'd like to introduce you to someone. Every good book contains a story, and every story needs a hero. Our hero's name is Adrian. He runs a digital agency in Bristol, UK, called Treadmill.

Adrian is fictitious, but his situation, and many of the challenges he faces, will be familiar to you. He's not based on any one person, nor Treadmill on a single agency. They're a combination of some of the people and businesses I've observed, met and worked with over the years. There's also some of my own experiences in Adrian's story.

Meet Adrian

Adrian was always fascinated with new technology. He started work selling computer hardware and began building websites in his spare time. As his knowledge and confidence grew, he quit his job to become a freelance web designer. After about 18 months, Adrian found himself with too much work. With encouragement from his wife, Sarah, Adrian employed his first member of staff and Treadmill was born!

The agency's first couple of years were tough. Their clients were small local businesses whose expectations were often bigger than their budgets. In time, Adrian secured a couple of larger clients. He employed more people and began offering more services. Treadmill became a full-service digital agency.

As the business grew, Sarah started working part-time overseeing finance and HR. In the early days, Treadmill grew rapidly, but in recent years it has stalled. They have a team of 10 now, but revenue has been about the same for the past three years. They work with a variety of clients of different sizes and across many sectors.

Treadmill makes a profit, but it's a lot less than what Adrian would like. He feels he does a lot of work and problem-solving for the returns the business generates. He often tells Sarah he could make the same money freelancing for other people.

Now he has a team working for him, Adrian misses the buzz of working directly with clients. He feels his input is no longer required and clients only seem to speak to him when there's a problem. He worries that other people in the agency now know more about digital marketing than he does. He's lost confidence.

Adrian has never enjoyed managing people, but that's what he spends most of his time doing these days. Ideally he wants a management team to run the agency for him. He has two senior people, but he can't trust them to run the business yet. They still have a lot to learn. Despite this, he worries that they will leave. The prospect of having to recruit for one of these roles again frightens him.

For some time now, Adrian has been thinking about selling his agency. He's been dreaming about setting up a different type of business. He's got a few friends that are running tech start-ups, or selling products through e-commerce. Treadmill is more successful than they are, but Adrian is strangely envious of them.

He used to enjoy running his agency, but now it feels as if it's harder work than it's ever been. It's like he's riding a rollercoaster. One day he's elated as they've won a new client, the next he's going down a dip as somebody has handed in their notice. Working under this pressure is very stressful. It's even been putting a strain on Adrian's relationship with Sarah.

In 2020, Adrian's rollercoaster plunged into a dark tunnel. COVID-19 changed the world. Treadmill survived, and even won a few new clients, but Adrian had to take on some debt to support the business. He's fiercely proud of what he's achieved at Treadmill, but he doesn't feel in control of his business. He feels as if it controls him.

STANDSTILL Agencies

You won't be in exactly the same position as Adrian, but some of his story will be familiar to you. He may also remind you of friends or other agency owners you know. Like all of us, Adrian has recently had to guide his business through the most challenging period of our lifetimes. Treadmill has survived, but what happens now?

Adrian is facing the same industry and global challenges as the rest of us, but Treadmill's problems are more acute. There are some great digital agencies out there. Some are brilliant. Sadly, there are thousands more, like Treadmill, that are average, mediocre, and well, ordinary. (Sorry Adrian!)

Treadmill is what I call a STANDSTILL agency. The term isn't meant to be derogatory. Most of these firms are decent businesses, they've just stagnated. Adrian knows his business had issues well before the pandemic, but he doesn't know how to change things. The agency has grown to a certain level, but it's plateaued. Adrian has plateaued with it. He finds himself having to run harder and harder only for Treadmill to stand still.

The Problem with STANDSTILL Agencies

STANDSTILL agency owners have many problems to deal with in the course of running their businesses. These agencies have three perennial challenges though:

1. *How do we win and keep more profitable clients?*
2. *How do we recruit and keep the best people?*
3. *How do I keep my motivation for running the agency?*

These are the things that keep agency owners awake at night. They may well be troubling you.

Let's take a look at each of them in a little more detail.

1. ***Winning and keeping profitable clients***

New Business, Business Development or Sales and Marketing. Whatever you call it, it's the most talked about issue in every marketing agency I've worked with. It's also the area where agencies completing my free online Agency Health Check[7] consistently score themselves the lowest.

Winning new business is a challenge for all but the most high-profile firms. All agencies want more clients and more revenue. But finding them is time consuming, frustrating and costly. Retaining them can be equally challenging.

STANDSTILL agencies don't help themselves. They make critical mistakes:

Poor positioning – STANDSTILL agencies prefer to offer a wide variety of services rather than focus on a specific skill. They believe that breadth of knowledge is more attractive than deep expertise. They take a similar approach to their client base. They think broadly appealing to many is better than appealing strongly to a targeted few.

Poor marketing – Most marketing agencies are desperately poor at marketing themselves. Marketing their own business becomes an afterthought. STANDSTILL agencies get distracted by other things. Delivering client workload

7. www.beyond-noise.com/agency-health-check/

they do some marketing, they talk more about themselves and their services, rather than their clients. They focus on the services they offer rather than the problems they solve.

Silver bullet – STANDSTILL agency owners abdicate responsibility for finding new clients at the first opportunity. They try to find a great 'New Business Director'. Somebody who doesn't want to run their own agency but is happy to work on commission to find clients for somebody else. Do these people even exist?

LBS (Leaky Bucket Syndrome) – Whilst STANDSTILL agencies focus on winning and onboarding new clients, their existing relationships suffer. New clients walk in the front door, whilst existing clients walk out of the back. Winning new clients is important, but client retention and development is vital. They say attraction is the battle, but retention is the war. You must do both to grow. That said, it's often overlooked that developing existing clients is your biggest and easiest form of incremental business.

2. ***Recruiting and keeping the best people***

Clients are oxygen for agencies, but it's people that are their lifeblood. People provide the knowledge and skills that enable you to generate revenue. They're your biggest asset, but also one of your biggest headaches.

Most agency owners face a battle to find, recruit, manage, motivate and keep staff. STANDSTILL agencies find it particularly difficult. They don't have the money or profile to attract the best people and they face competition from those that do.

More competition – People have far more options now than when I started my agency career. Clients have in-house teams. Tech companies have a huge demand for people with digital skills. Anybody can freelance or set up their own business. These changes impact all agencies, but the best talent goes to the best agencies. STANDSTILL agencies find themselves at the back of the queue.

Less desirable – Agencies in general are not as attractive employers as they once were. Agency culture once had an edge over other industries. At the start of my career, they were aspirational places to be. An alternative to the stuffy environment of a corporate office. Today, many client brands provide better perks, more innovative spaces, and more modern ways of working than agencies. It's not that agencies are bad employment options, but they're less of a pull than they once were. STANDSTILL agencies even less so.

Different attitudes – Work/life balance has become far more important to people in recent times. Agencies have historically called for longer hours and more commitment than some industries. The agency business model is coming under increasing strain from changing attitudes to work. It's not only about long hours either; flexibility and home working have been normalised by the pandemic. Whilst it's possible for agencies to work in a distributed way, is it desirable? There are implications for culture, teamwork, client service, and learning and development.

3. *Finding and keeping your motivation*

Clients and great people are vital to growing an agency business. Neither of these things are really what makes an agency a success though. The single most important factor in growing an agency is the person reading this book. You, the agency leader.

There is nobody more pivotal to the success of a business than its leader. Natural talent for leadership is important, but what's even more critical is how you grow and develop. Natural leadership ability and enthusiasm fuels the agency in the early days, but when the agency starts to grow, leaders must grow with it. Not everyone can – or wants to – make this transition to running a bigger business. Not everybody can sustain their passion and momentum.

STANDSTILL agency leaders usually find the early days fun and exciting. They grow the business and have some success. Unfortunately, many soon reach a point where they lose their enthusiasm and drive. Let's take a look at some of the reasons why this happens.

Accidental ownership – Often, digital agency owners don't set out to run a business; they grow them without a clear plan or direction. STANDSTILL agency leaders often lack experience themselves. For many, managing people is not why they entered the industry. The challenges of managing people and leading a business are thrust upon them. They don't always embrace or even like these new roles.

Growing pains – They struggle to adapt as the agency grows and they become less effective and more frustrated. They must delegate more and trust people to run parts of the business for them. They can't get everybody together in a room like they used to. They have to give people more autonomy and don't know everything that is going on at all times. For many STANDSTILL agency owners growth – both business and personal – can be a challenge.

Driven to distraction – As a business grows it can become less enjoyable to run. It feels more like operating a machine than playing a game you enjoy. The energy and risk-taking of the early days are replaced by the need for direction and coordination. Daily routines for the founder(s) become less fun and more predictable. They themselves can become less important to the daily operations of the business. STANDSTILL leaders get distracted and demotivated. They can start to lose sight of their role in the agency.

From STANDSTILL to STANDOUT

Whilst you've been reading this chapter you will have been asking yourself an obvious question: 'Am I running a STANDSTILL agency?' You may be convinced of the answer, or still be undecided. You may see a lot of yourself in Adrian, or maybe just a little.

Whatever your response, you've actually been asking yourself the wrong question. It's not important whether you're running a STANDSTILL agency. The important thing you should be asking yourself is: 'How do I build a STANDOUT agency?'

The reality is that you're probably not a STANDSTILL agency, but you're not the best agency in the world either. You're likely to be somewhere in between. Whatever your current situation, maintaining the status quo is not a good strategy. What you must do is keep improving and keep growing. The world is changing and so must you.

One of my favourite mantras is 'if you're not growing, you're dying'. You have to keep evolving, adapting and growing if you want to stay ahead. A word of warning though, I find many agency owners are obsessed with growth, but in the wrong way. They consider anything that isn't growing ***bigger*** to be a failure.

Growth is not always about getting bigger. It doesn't have to always reveal itself on a spreadsheet. Growth is not only about size, revenue or profit figures. You don't have to always be growing bigger, but you do need to be growing. You need to be developing your offer and your skills, enhancing your culture and refining your proposition. You and your people must always be learning and developing.

STANDSTILL agencies come in all shapes and sizes. They're not just smaller agencies. They're not just the ones that can't break the £1 million turnover mark. They do share some common traits though. They lack ambition. They seem happy to blend in and make up the numbers. Like Treadmill, they're nothing special.

If you struggle to attract and retain clients, if you find it difficult to find and keep the best people, or if you find your own motivation for running the business is not always what it should be, you have a problem. You may not necessarily be a STANDSTILL agency, but you do have an opportunity. You too can become a STANDOUT agency. The next chapter is going to introduce you to seven levers. They're collectively known as the STANDOUT agency R.O.A.D.M.A.P. These principles have helped many agencies like yours on the road to STANDOUT status. They can do the same for you.

CHAPTER 3

STANDOUT AGENCIES

The difference between mediocrity and excellence is often a matter of effort.

Diana Waring, Author

As we have seen, there are many reasons why an agency might find themselves in STANDSTILL mode. It can also happen at any time. Some people need help to get their business off the ground. Many start off well but find it more difficult as their agency grows. Others run their agency for several years only to find themselves in a comfort zone. Sometimes, their business performance dips and they realise their agency is uncompetitive. More often, they become frustrated that both they and their agency are not reaching their full potential.

So, what is the alternative? What is a STANDOUT agency, and why would you want your agency to be one?

STANDOUT agencies are not the biggest. They rarely have the most services or the widest experience. They might not work with clients that are household names. They don't even have to be recognised by a wide audience themselves.

STANDOUT agencies, as the name suggests, draw attention to themselves. They get noticed. These agencies are in a battle for attention like everyone else, but they do something the others don't. They attract, but they also repel.

These agencies alienate some clients, prospective employees, even partners and suppliers. Some people decide a particular STANDOUT agency isn't for them. This is a good thing, but it's a difficult concept for STANDSTILL agencies to grasp. They have a herd mentality. They want to fit in. They want to be liked by everybody and be an option for everyone.

STANDOUT agencies set out to polarise. They separate those people that are for them and those that are not for them. They force people to have a strong opinion of them and in doing so they help people make a decision. They get people to choose if they are interested in working with them or not. In a sea of sameness and a sector of mediocrity, STANDOUT agencies push people off the fence. They, well, stand out.

If you want to own an agency that you enjoy running and growing, a business that attracts and retains clients and top talent, then you need to create a STANDOUT agency. So how do you move from STANDSTILL to STANDOUT? Let me introduce you to the STANDOUT agency R.O.A.D.M.A.P.

The future doesn't belong to the mediocre. In a world where the pace of change and volume of competition will only continue to increase, standing out really is the only option. The R.O.A.D.M.A.P. is a blueprint for enabling your agency to stand out in a sector where there is huge demand for digital expertise but where there is also massive oversupply.

Only the best digital agencies will thrive. To be the best you must focus. Focus on what you're best at, who you're best for and communicating why you're the best in the most compelling way.

Before we get into how you can make your agency stand out, let's take a look closer at what you have to gain. We know STANDOUT agencies seek to separate themselves from the competition, but what are the benefits of doing this? What advantages do STANDOUT agency owners have?

Why STANDOUT?

There are many benefits of becoming a STANDOUT agency, but three rise above all others:

1. STANDOUT agencies are more *visible*.

Oscar Wilde said: 'There is only one thing in life worse than being talked about, and that is not being talked about.' There is no point being brilliant if nobody can see, hear or experience it. STANDOUT agencies create awareness. They're known. They build their profile amongst their clients, prospects and talent base. They invest in their own marketing and believe in what they're doing. They become well known and a recognised name. How do they do this? They do it by differentiating themselves, but not in a way you might expect. They don't call themselves a wacky name or make weird and wonderful claims about what they do. Nor do they try to list as many services they provide as possible. They do the opposite. They differentiate themselves by narrowing their scope. To become famous is difficult. It's even harder to become known for many things. To become famous amongst a certain group, or groups, of people is much more achievable. It's easier still if that fame is based on specific expertise.

2. STANDOUT agencies are more *desirable.*

These agencies don't compete with their peers, they compete with themselves. They aim to become experts and the very best in their field. They have a desire to deliver results and make a tangible difference to the lives of the people they work with. STANDOUT agencies are specialists. They're not just available, they're desirable.

Owners of these agencies believe in being the very best at what they do, not being good all-rounders. They create clarity in what their agency stands for, who it works with, what it delivers and where it is going. They set them apart from the STANDSTILL agencies. They are more desirable to clients and prospective employees. They attract clients, and people to want to come and work with them and for them. STANDOUT agency owners are more connected and in control of their business. They have greater confidence in their firm's offer and their abilities. They want to grow a great business, not exit and do something else.

3. STANDOUT agencies are more *valuable.*

The purpose of becoming more visible and desirable is not to make the agency famous. It's not to satisfy the ego of the agency owner either. It's to make the agency more valuable. STANDOUT agencies are more valuable as they're more profitable and enjoyable to run. The purpose of any business is to create and deliver value to generate profit. But value should not be measured purely in monetary terms. A STANDOUT agency is valuable to all its stakeholders in different ways. For clients, they're a trusted partner that helps them to grow their business. For employees, they're a great place to work, and a great place to learn. For the agency owner, the value is in creating a business that can generate an income, but also be an asset that one day has the potential to be valuable to somebody else.

STANDOUT Agencies are not ...

I've explained a lot about what STANDOUT agencies are, but before we go any further, let me also make it clear what they're not.

Not a quick fix – Building a STANDOUT agency is not a quick process. Neither is it a quick fix to solve your immediate problems or challenges. Creating a STANDOUT agency will take time, determination and perseverance.

Not get rich quick – There is an increasing number of agency gurus talking about how to grow agencies. Many advertise courses on Facebook that will change the fortunes of your agency overnight. They propose to make you a millionaire living the high life (whatever that means). You can even generate new clients every month whilst sitting on a beach. If that's what you were looking for from this book, then I'm sorry but you're going to be disappointed. Creating a STANDOUT agency will lead to your agency becoming valuable and maybe even a target for acquisition. If that happens for you then I'll be delighted. I'll be equally happy if this book empowers you to make your agency more successful and you become more motivated and enjoy running it.

Not the loudest – I speak to many agency owners who might want their businesses to stand out, but they don't want to stand out themselves. They didn't enter the industry to become a minor celebrity or spend their time recording YouTube videos. I understand and empathise with this view. As you'll learn later, it's vital for all agency leaders to play a major role in the marketing of the agency. Yet, becoming a STANDOUT agency is not about shouting the loudest or having the biggest profile. Standing out is about being the most focused, not about being the most famous.

Not the biggest – STANDOUT agencies are not the biggest in their sector, or even in their local area. For too long, digital agencies have been obsessed with growth, or scaling, as people seem to prefer to call it. STANDOUT agencies aim to be the best, not the biggest.

Not (completely) unique – We're all unique in some way and so is every digital agency. But becoming a STANDOUT agency doesn't need you to be completely different from everybody else. That's an impossible task. You're already unique, you just need to work harder at being recognised for it. The R.O.A.D.M.A.P. will be your guide.

The STANDOUT Agency R.O.A.D.M.A.P.

The STANDOUT agency R.O.A.D.M.A.P. is a framework for growth constructed from seven principles. These principles are the building blocks to move you from STANDSTILL to STANDOUT.

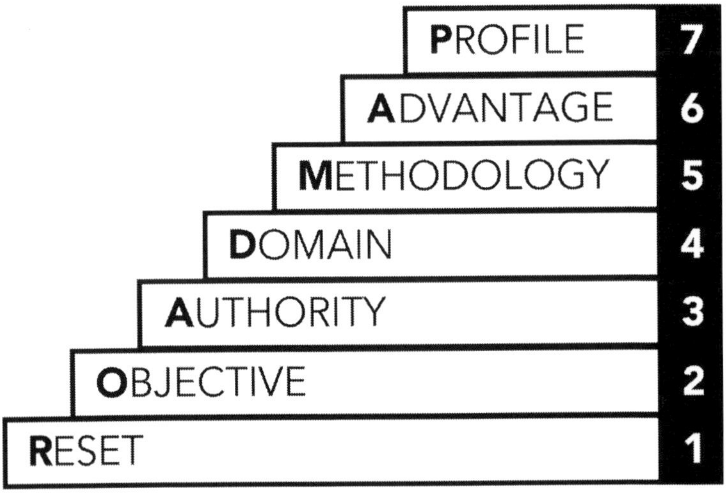

Over the next seven chapters I'm going to explain the R.O.A.D.M.A.P. to you in more detail. Before we start though, here's an introduction to each principle.

1. RESET – Master your Mindset

The process starts with you, the agency owner. In the next chapter you're going to learn how important the right mindset is in building a STANDOUT agency. Your personal motivation is the starting point.

STANDOUT agencies are led by people who are focused, motivated and engaged. They're motivated by building their agency, not hoping to sell it. Like STANDSTILL agency owners, STANDOUT leaders are not happy. But they're not happy for a different reason. They're unfulfilled. They want to better. They want to run an extraordinary business. They don't want to be just another digital agency making up the numbers.

Whatever point you are at in your agency journey, if you want to make a change, then that change starts with you, the agency owner. You're going to need to reset your thinking and master your mindset. Find out more in the next chapter.

2. OBJECTIVE – Power your Purpose

The journey to STANDOUT status is one you can't complete alone. You're going to need a great team around you. In Chapter 5 you're going to learn how having a clear purpose is a vital component in building a great team.

STANDOUT agencies rely on attracting the best people. Recruiting, motivating and retaining great people is vital to their success. To do this consistently and effectively, STANDOUT agencies don't just stand out, they stand for something. They're on a mission beyond just making money for their owners. Financial success is important, but these agencies exist to achieve something more. They focus on making a difference, not just being different. You must have an objective that inspires and motivates your people, your clients and yourself. You need to power your purpose.

3. AUTHORITY – Sell your Specialism

In Chapter 6 you're going to learn why depth of expertise is more important than breadth of services. To be a STANDOUT agency, you need to accept that less is more. You need to be an expert in a specific skill.

STANDOUT agencies are specialists not generalists. They're more respected, valued and highly paid because of this. They narrow their focus to gain visibility more quickly and easily. They're committed to being the best at what they do and strive to continually improve and develop their skills and knowledge.

To build a STANDOUT agency you'll need to become known for being an authority in a specific area. You must be exceptional at one thing and make sure everybody knows about it. You need to sell your specialism.

4. DOMAIN – Choose your Clients

You can't serve everybody everywhere. You must choose a domain to operate in. Chapter 7 will show you why it's so important to target and dominate a specific client audience.

STANDOUT agencies have something STANDSTILL agencies don't – a target market. They dedicate themselves to a type of client. They become experts in the specific problems their target clients have. Then they commit to providing the best possible solutions that solve them.

Having a specific domain not only helps you win business, it also gives you more power and control. It turbocharges both your new business opportunities and your effectiveness. To stand out you need to choose your clients.

5. METHODOLOGY – Productise your Process

You don't have to want to be the biggest agency in the world. You do need to be able to scale. In Chapter 8 you're going to learn why your processes are so important and why you need to standardise them.

STANDOUT agencies are service businesses but they're not service providers. They sell productised services, not time billed by the hour. They have a defined methodology, which makes what they do more tangible and helps them scale their businesses more effectively.

If you want to grow your agency without constantly adding headcount, you need to standardise what you do. You must create a method and productise your processes. STANDOUT agencies standardise their services so that they can more easily learn, refine and improve them. This chapter will show you how you can do the same.

6. ADVANTAGE – Demonstrate your Difference

You can't just say you're different and expect people to believe it. You must have a competitive advantage. In Chapter 9 you're going to learn how to define and communicate how you make a difference by constructing a clear Value Proposition.

STANDOUT agencies attract more clients more easily because they make a discernible difference to their businesses. They don't make claims about how they're different like STANDSTILL agencies. Their goal is to create value for their clients by doing something different. Something their competitors can't, or don't, do.

You must be able to communicate how you can make a difference to your clients' lives if you want them to buy into and from you. The penultimate principle will help you capture your competitive advantage and demonstrate your difference.

7. PROFILE – Build your Brand

To build a great business you need to build a great brand. All the other principles amount to nothing if nobody knows about you or your agency. In Chapter 10 you're going to learn about the power of branding, and why your agency needs more than one brand to succeed.

STANDOUT agencies are high-profile brands. They have more confidence in themselves and their abilities. They know a great reputation attracts great people and a strong brand brings better clients. Their leaders invest not only in marketing their business but also in marketing themselves.

A high profile helps agencies stand out, win business and attract talent. You must invest time, money and effort over the long-term to build your brand. This principle is far from being the final piece in the R.O.A.D.M.A.P., it should be placed at the very heart of your agency journey.

Using the R.O.A.D.M.A.P.

A good strategy articulates what must change, why it must change, and in what sequence the change should happen. There is an order to the R.O.A.D.M.A.P. but becoming a STANDOUT agency is not a linear process. Neither is it a project that can be executed quickly. It is a journey and a long-term commitment.

Like any journey, getting off to a good start is vital. Every person reading this book will be at a different stage of developing their agency. Whatever your situation, you should start at the beginning of the R.O.A.D.M.A.P. The next chapter, RESET, is the foundation principle. It is the starting point on which the rest of the blueprint is built.

The other six principles of the R.O.A.D.M.A.P. can be deployed out of sequence if you wish. You don't have to address each one in turn. You might find one that resonates with you more than others that you want to focus on, or ideally, you might decide to implement more than one principle at a time. However you approach it, I hope you enjoy learning about the principles in the next seven chapters.

Can't wait to get started? Then read on.

PART 2

THE STANDOUT AGENCY R.O.A.D.M.A.P.

CHAPTER 4

RESET

I'm here to build something for the long-term.
Anything else is a distraction.

Mark Zuckerberg

Principle #1 RESET – Master your Mindset

The first principle in our R.O.A.D.M.A.P. is RESET. The journey to STANDOUT status starts with you, the agency owner, and particularly your mindset. To become a STANDOUT agency, you will need to change your thinking and approach. Having the right mentality at the top of the agency is critical to success. You must master your mindset.

STANDSTILL agencies are managed by people who are dissatisfied, demotivated and distracted. They work hard, often too hard, but they're not focused on building their business or creating something distinctive. They're preoccupied with other things like selling and doing something different.

STANDOUT agencies are led by people who are focused, motivated and engaged. They have a different mindset. They're not happy with being just another digital agency. They want to create something special and enjoy doing it. They're motivated by building and growing, not selling and exiting.

In this chapter you're going to learn:

- The importance of having the right mindset.
- How beliefs shape your attitude.
- How clarity fuels your motivation.
- What STANDOUT agencies believe.

Life at a STANDSTILL

Adrian has developed a lot of negative beliefs about Treadmill and his situation. He's stressed and feels as if he's lost control of the agency. He thinks other people are more knowledgeable about digital marketing than he is, and he finds it a struggle to keep up. Adrian has stopped learning and growing. He's become very set in his ways.

Despite his success, Adrian looks at other people's businesses with envy. He believes these companies must be easier to run than Treadmill. Rather than thinking about how he can develop his agency, he believes his future lies elsewhere. He has many projects and side hustles on the go. He's full of ideas, but he's often distracted. He gives up easily when a project has a setback, and moves on to something new.

Adrian often blames other people when things go wrong. He doesn't take feedback well and gets very defensive. He even finds it difficult to listen to Sarah when she is trying to help him. Part of his problem is that he struggles to delegate. He doesn't like to think other people can do something as well as he can.

If Adrian is to make Treadmill into a STANDOUT agency, the first thing he must do is change his mindset. But how can he adapt his beliefs and reset? Where will he find the motivation?

A STANDOUT Mindset

Your mindset is your attitude and way of thinking. It's determined by your environment, health and experiences. But it's particularly influenced by your beliefs. It affects what you think, how you feel and what you do. It shapes your habits, how you live and how you run your agency.

Everybody reading this book is at a different stage of their agency journey. You're all individuals with different experiences, beliefs and attitudes. Some of you will identify with the situation Adrian finds himself in after many years running Treadmill, others will have less experience than Adrian but have more energy and enthusiasm.

Whilst you're all different, you have at least one thing in common:

You're not satisfied with your agency and/or your role within it.

How do I know this? You wouldn't be reading this book if everything in your business was perfect. That's not to suggest you are desperately unhappy or underperforming. Some of you might be, but I guess the majority of you simply want more. You don't feel as if you or your agency have reached your full potential yet. Your ambitions are still to be realised and you're not enjoying running your business, or reaping the rewards of it, as much as you think you should.

If the start of the 2020 decade has taught us anything, it's that life is unpredictable. It's far too short and uncertain to be doing something you don't enjoy. You must run an agency that excites and fulfils you. After all, if you don't enjoy something, why do it?

Riding the Rollercoaster

Mindset and confidence play a big part in building a STANDOUT agency. An agency owner friend of mine spoke for many when he told me: 'One minute I think I've cracked it and I have the best agency in the world, another day I feel like I don't know what I'm doing.' He's not alone and I told him so. This is a common feeling amongst agency owners. I've felt like that many times.

All businesses are emotional journeys. It's normal to have ups and downs. But running an agency can be a particularly unpredictable rollercoaster ride. One day you can win a big pitch and feel on top of the world, the next you can have a key client resign and suddenly an important piece of your business is in jeopardy. No matter how experienced you are, there always seems to be a surprise around the corner.

Whilst running an agency is often challenging, it's rarely dull. And the challenges change over time. Many agency people start their business having honed their own skills in an agency or as a freelancer. Once they own a business, they find themselves not doing the things they love and enjoy anymore. They're managing people and clients rather than designing or coding.

MY STORY – In at the deep end

Buying my agency was the best thing I ever did, but it was a baptism of fire. I'd worked in the business for two years before we completed our MBO. In that time, I'd been responsible for a large team and supported the founder in running the business. Even so, from the day of the buyout my partners and I embarked on a very different journey.

We had to adapt from being part of the team to leading the business. Our day-to-day roles changed almost overnight. The weight of responsibility was a shock. The skills we learned before we bought the business stood us in good stead, but we had a lot to learn about leading an agency.

I soon realised that there is a big difference between running a business and growing a business. I also started to understand that keeping positive and motivated was a different challenge when, as a business owner, you are so much more emotionally – and financially – invested in its success.

Becoming demotivated or disillusioned with your business can happen to anybody at any time. Your agency may have more complex problems now than when you first started out. You may find you are lacking the business acumen required to run a growing business. You may be struggling with a particular aspect of running the agency that you don't feel suited to or particularly enjoy. External events in your personal life, or the world at large, might test your resolve.

Whatever the reason, if you find yourself in this position, you must reset and engage the right mindset before doing anything else. Mindset is the foundation on which your success is built. This has always been the case, but it's particularly important given the turbulent times we live in.

Despite recent global events, we must remember that there has never been a more exciting time to run a business. Neither has it ever been easier. The demand for digital skills has never been higher. For those agencies ready to take advantage of them, the opportunities are greater than ever. Don't settle for mediocrity and be a STANDSTILL agency. Now is not the time for negativity, now is the time to get excited about your business again.

Believe in Yourself

Whilst it's easy for somebody to tell you to change your mindset, it can be difficult to do. It's particularly hard if you've been thinking the same way for a long period of time. Your mindset is shaped by your beliefs, and they're usually deeply ingrained.

Contrary to popular opinion, your beliefs are not your values. They might influence your values, but they're not one and the same thing. Our values represent what is important to us. Beliefs are what we consider to be true. Beliefs are influenced mainly by two things; what people tell you and your own personal experiences.

Beliefs can be a positive and a negative force in your life. They can be self-limiting and hold you back, or they help you achieve things you never thought possible. How you balance them determines your mindset.

Stanford University psychologist, Dr Carol Dweck, has spent her career analysing influences on personal achievement and success. She's a particular advocate of the power of mindset. Dweck believes that it's not just our abilities and talent that bring us success, it's whether we approach life with what she refers to as a Growth or Fixed Mindset.

People with a Growth Mindset believe basic abilities and skills can be developed through dedication and hard work. They consider brains and talent to be just the starting point. They embrace feedback and failure as an opportunity to learn and grow.

By contrast, people with a Fixed Mindset believe talent is innate, they avoid challenges, and they give up easily. They often see feedback as criticism. A Fixed Mindset limits growth and limits opportunities.

A Growth Mindset is a quest for constant learning. The desire to embrace challenges and persist in the face of obstacles. People with a Growth Mindset believe that effort is the path to mastery. They learn from feedback, criticism and mistakes. They also find lessons in the experiences of others.

As a people business, an agency must be driven and inspired by its leadership. If they themselves don't want to be the best at what they do, the agency will never reach its full potential. To achieve this, agency leaders must be constantly growing and trying to improve themselves as well as their business.

STANDOUT agency owners resist the desire to always look smart. They embrace the desire to learn. In an industry built on knowledge, expertise and egos, this can be difficult for some people to accept. The fact that you're reading this book, already suggests that you're willing to grow yourself as well as your agency. This is a great start.

Keeping Motivated

Changing your beliefs and mindset can take a lot of soul-searching and determination. Sometimes, even finding the motivation to do this can be a challenge. Agencies are a team sport, and all great teams need great leaders. It's impossible to motivate others if you're lacking in motivation yourself.

If you find yourself in this situation, I have a secret that can help you to push through it. It's something I've learned from running my own agency and from working with others. It's based on a simple truth:

Motivation comes from clarity

When people lack motivation they try to look for inspiration from lots of different sources. This often only serves to bring them more complexity and confusion. To find and maintain your motivation, what you really need is clarity. The clearer you are on where you are going, the easier it is to motivate yourself to change. After all, the key to getting what you want is knowing what you want.

Clarity is achieved by understanding three things:

1. Where are you now?
2. Where do you want to be?
3. What is holding you back?

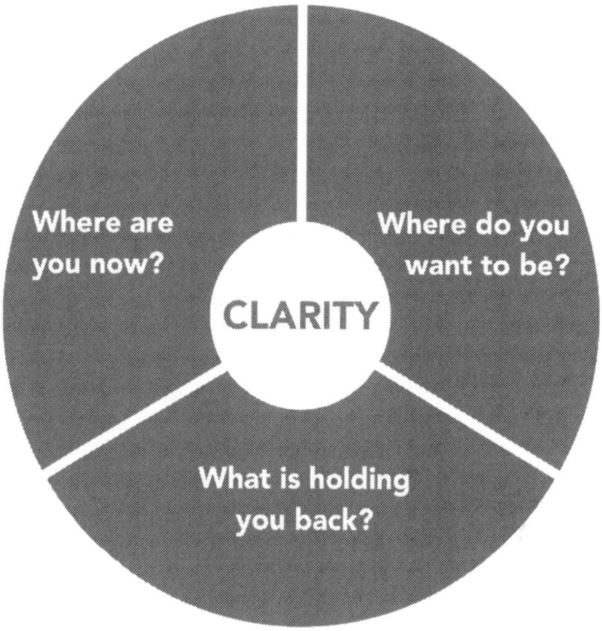

If you're clear on what you're doing, where you're heading and how you're going to get there, you're motivated. Often the task ahead of you isn't any easier, but clarity makes it seem more achievable. Your motivation and your mindset get a huge boost from more clarity.

EXERCISE

Take a piece of paper and give yourself 30 minutes in a quiet space. Write the following three headings at the top of the page.

1. Where am I now?

2. Where do I want to be?

3. What is holding me back?

Now jot down as many things that come into your head under each heading. Keep it related to your agency and business, or expand it out to life in general, it's your choice.

What do you learn from the exercise?

What can you change today that will help you overcome what is holding you back?

What mindset can you adopt to make those changes easier?

Bigger is Not Always Better

Having a Growth Mindset doesn't mean you have to be obsessed with growing your agency. STANDOUT agencies don't have to be big, and they don't have to be constantly getting bigger. Agencies I work with broadly fall into two categories.

1. **Lifestyle** – An agency with up to 15 people that has potential to reach more than £1 million in gross profit. These agencies can provide their owners with a good income. In many cases they can be easier and more enjoyable to run.

2. **Growth** – An agency of between 15 and 50 people that can deliver up to £3 million gross profit. These agencies bring bigger revenue that can lead to bigger profits. They also come with bigger challenges.

Often, STANDSTILL agencies fall somewhere in between these two classifications. They're trapped in a no man's land where the owner doesn't want a Lifestyle business, but they're too small and don't have the knowledge, processes and systems in place to make the leap to Growth.

You may decide making such a leap is not for you. This is perfectly OK. There are around 6 million small and medium-sized enterprises (SMEs) in the UK. Around 75% of them don't employ anybody other than the owner-director. Even if you only have one employee on your payroll, you're already in the top 25% of SMEs in the UK. There's nothing wrong with being a Lifestyle agency. You may be very happy with a more manageable business with a tight-knit agile team.

Most entrepreneurs talk about making money. What people really crave though is not money but freedom. Money is worthless in itself, it's the freedom it can give you that gives it its value. But what's your definition of freedom? For some people it might be being able to buy their own home so that they can move out of their parents' house. For others it's a private jet so they don't have to queue for commercial airlines with the rest of us.

With both a Lifestyle agency and a Growth agency it's possible for the agency owner to earn £100,000 a year, or more. The question is, do you want to earn that running a small team and doing lots of the work yourself? Or are you more excited by having a large team of people working for you? Is the agency something that gives you the freedom to work for yourself and make your own decisions? Or are you driven by the desire to build an asset and achieve a big payday through a sale? It's not impossible to sell Lifestyle agencies, but the opportunities and valuations are usually more limited.

You have a choice about whether you choose Lifestyle or Growth agency. Whichever you decide, don't accept mediocrity. You must make it a STANDOUT agency.

EXERCISE

Answer the following questions. If you have a business partner(s), ask them to do the same exercise without you, then meet to compare notes.

- Do you want a Lifestyle or Growth agency?
- What does this mean for you?
- How much money do you want to earn?
- How many people do you want to employ?
- What will it take to get you from where you are now to achieve your ambition?
- Does your business partner(s) agree and share your vision?
- Has your ambition changed over the last 12 months?

STANDOUT Beliefs

The mindset of STANDOUT agency owners is influenced by three core beliefs they share. You may find these controversial; they conflict with what many people in the industry advocate or are led to believe.

The STANDOUT core beliefs are:

1. Specialist over Generalist

STANDOUT agencies believe in specialism over generalism. They aim to thrive in a segment of the market, not struggle to survive amongst the hordes of other agencies. They narrow the competitive field rather than try to compete with it.

Digital marketing has flourished through three main technological advancements: the internet, smartphones, big data. Many see the next advancement as artificial intelligence. With this technology has come a myriad of applications and channels for marketing. There are over 40 speciality areas of digital marketing today and the list is growing.

Yet, despite this scale and complexity, STANDSTILL agencies try to spread themselves too thinly. People like Adrian believe in breadth. They like being able to do things more for more clients. They lack focus and would rather offer a broad range of services to a broad range of clients.

With so many agencies, channels and increasing complexity, the power is moving to the specialist not the generalist. This will be even more important in the future.

The market for digital agency services will become even more polarised.

There will still be a demand for general digital services amongst smaller clients. STANDSTILL agencies will continue to try and juggle building websites alongside search engine optimisation (SEO) and paid advertising etc. But the relationship between smaller clients and agencies will become increasingly price-sensitive and frustrating. They'll find it harder to make a profit.

STANDOUT agencies operate at the other end of the market. They focus on working with larger clients as subject-matter experts. They support their clients' own digital resources and are paid for their thinking as well as their ability to execute. They provide extra knowledge as well as sense-checking work done elsewhere.

EXERCISE

Answer the following questions:

- What services do you say you provide for clients?
- Which ones are your true areas of expertise?
- Which ones make the biggest difference for clients?
- Which ones are you famous for?
- Which do you personally like or enjoy the most?
- What is your specialism?

2. Distinctive over Different

STANDOUT agencies believe in being distinctive over being different. Conventional wisdom tells us that to stand out you have to be unique. The industry is full of agencies trying – and failing – to live up to this. Many STANDSTILL agencies try hard to be unique, but they invariably end up looking the same and saying the same things.

If your agency has something completely unique, something that no other agency can do, you are extremely lucky. Do everything you can to use it to help you stand out. Be honest with yourself though. If you think your unique attribute is the fact that you've won some awards, or that you have a great set of people, or that you are results-focused, please think again. These things may all be true but they're hygiene factors. I'm not saying they're worthless, they're just so me-too that they make your agency blend in rather than stand out.

In such a crowded market you must differentiate, but STANDOUT agencies know that to do so you don't have to be unique, you have to be distinctive. Distinctiveness is not about trying to find unique selling points (USPs). That concept was created when the first TV advertisements were broadcast. In today's hyper-connected world, if you do discover or create something unique, it rarely stays that way for long.

Distinctiveness is about maximising and promoting lots of smaller qualities rather than one big one. It's branding not marketing. Distinctiveness is achieved using brand assets such as brand name, logos, colours, messaging, methodology, profile, etc. These assets help clients, prospects, and people in general, easily identify, recall, and buy into the agency.

Digital marketers have become obsessed with tactical marketing, technology and immediate results. They ignore the power of branding. Many of the great advertising agencies used it to great effect to build their brands. Saatchi & Saatchi famously carved their 'Nothing is Impossible' mantra into the steps of their London offices. They focused as much on building their own brand as they did on their clients. I'm not saying we should go back to the Mad Men era, but even in the world we live in today we can still learn from the past.

STANDOUT agencies build distinctive brands that are recognisable and memorable. These qualities increase the visibility and value of their agency. It makes them easier for clients to recognise, recall and buy.

To be a STANDOUT agency you don't have to be unique, but you do have to be distinctive. You must create a distinction that other agencies cannot easily claim, replicate or match, and amplify it through your brand.

EXERCISE

Answer the following questions:

- What claims do you make about your agency?
- Are they unique?
- Are they differentiating?
- Are they distinctive?

3. Today over Tomorrow

STANDOUT agencies believe in focusing on today not obsessing over tomorrow. In his book *The 7 Habits of Highly Effective People*, Stephen R. Covey introduces the principle of 'start with the end in mind'. It's a great book, but a word of warning – it's a concept that is massively overplayed and misinterpreted in the agency world.

STANDSTILL agency owners spend far too much time thinking about the future and exit planning. They set themselves a target for when they want to sell their business and for how much. Usually, these timeframes and valuations are overly ambitious. They ignore other important factors in selling an agency (and the fact that agencies are very difficult to sell).

Rather than foster the right mindset, this is counter-productive. I've met people running agencies for less than 12 months who have talked to me enthusiastically about their plans to eventually exit. Why would you start a business to then spend your time thinking about getting out?

Having a vision and planning ahead are crucial to running any successful business. Building a company that is also a valuable asset that may at some point be sold or passed on is sound business sense. However, agency owners obsessed with the end game – an exit – are missing the point. If I've learned anything in my time, it's that agency life really is about the journey, not the destination.

By all means have a vision, but don't think of the end goal as a sale. Think of it as creating a STANDOUT agency. Achieving this will get you a sale much quicker than planning for an exit that might never happen. The reality is that only a small minority of agency owners sell their business. Fewer still exit for the sums of money they dream about. There are many reasons for this, but at the core lies an inescapable truth; they're too ordinary. There's nothing special about their business. They're not bad, they're just not brilliant. Valuable to the current owner(s) but not that valuable to anybody else.

MY STORY – Jam tomorrow.

I admit that when I was running my agency I focused far too much on the future. I dreamed of what I wanted to achieve and if I'm honest, those dreams didn't involve the agency at all. They focused on selling the business to a large agency group in a multi-million pound deal.

My goal wasn't retirement, I was far too young and driven for that. I dreamed of 'doing something else'.

I have no regrets, but I admit that I didn't stop long or often enough to appreciate what I'd achieved. I didn't fully acknowledge what a great business I had the pleasure to be involved with. I wasn't enjoying the present. I was delaying my happiness for some sort of future event. Are you falling into the same mindset?

There's more to growing a business than growing to sell. Growth is not the goal; success is the goal and that isn't always measured by size or numbers. I don't judge agency owners on whether they sell their business, I judge them on how good the agency is. Building something that is profitable and enjoyable to run is the real objective. If your goals are rooted in selling, it's even less likely you'll ever achieve them. You'll know you have something valuable when you don't want to sell (even if you're approached).

The real enjoyment and rewards come from building an agency, not from selling it. STANDOUT agency owners actively pursue growth, but their leaders believe in enjoying the journey. They're present in the business, not wishing they were somewhere else. Agencies can be great cash flow generating machines if managed well. Realising value from a sale should be viewed as a bonus, not an objective. If you pursue it as an objective it will disrupt your mindset and your decision-making.

Building an agency takes 100% commitment. This is not the job for a serial entrepreneur or part-time business owner. Agencies are not 'set and forget' businesses. They take focus, commitment and incredible stamina. They're not a side hustle or a business you can step back from. They're a business you constantly need to lean into.

EXERCISE

Answer the following questions:

- What claims do you make about your agency?
- Do you enjoy running the agency?
- Money aside, what would make your working life better?
- What would make you happier and enjoy getting up on Monday mornings?
- What things that you have to do now do you not enjoy? Can these be delegated to somebody else? Can they be eliminated completely?

Chapter Summary – RESET

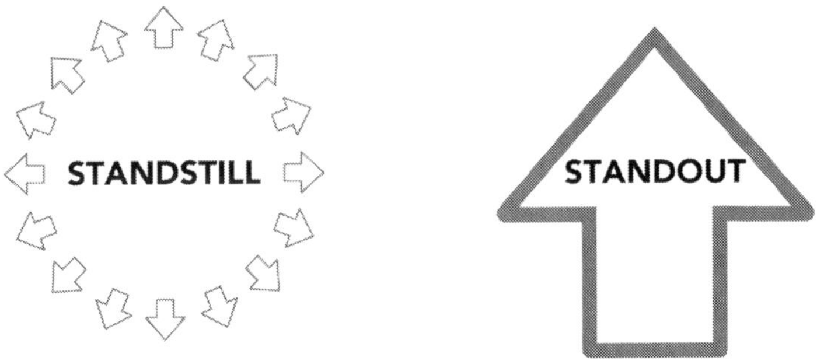

To build a STANDOUT agency you must master your mindset. You are the starting point. STANDOUT agency owners don't start with the end in mind, they start with the right mindset.

Your mindset is governed by your beliefs. Beliefs can be deeply ingrained and can be a positive or negative force in your journey. The key is to try and reduce or eliminate as many of the limiting beliefs as possible, whilst harnessing and utilising the positives. This is called cultivating a Growth Mindset.

There's never been a better time to reset. The key to mastering your mindset is clarity. Take stock and clarify where you are now and where you want to get to. You must have a vision and long-term goals for your agency. But you must also be motivated and have a passion for what you are trying to achieve in the short term.

There are two different agency approaches: Lifestyle and Growth. Whichever one you pursue, enjoy the journey of building your agency. Every business is a lifestyle business until you stop working in it.

CHAPTER 5

OBJECTIVE

Never start a business to make money, start a business to make a difference.

Marie Forleo, entrepreneur and author

PRINCIPLE #2 OBJECTIVE – Power your Purpose

To become a STANDOUT agency, you need to have the right mindset, but you'll need help from other people to achieve your objectives, and they'll need to be motivated by something other than your personal goals and making a profit.

The second principle in our R.O.A.D.M.A.P. is OBJECTIVE. To STANDOUT you need to stand for something. You need to power your purpose.

STANDSTILL agencies are managed for money. The main purpose of the agency is to generate profits for the owner(s). Their objective is to sell the business. The owners of these agencies struggle to create real engagement with their people and clients. This is not surprising. Their aspirations only serve to motivate and benefit them.

STANDOUT agencies are led with purpose. Their owners have financial goals, but they exist to make a difference to their clients, the people that work for them and even the wider world. they're purpose-driven. This inspires people. It creates one of the most powerful assets you can have in a people business – a unique and vibrant culture.

In this chapter you're going to learn:

- The importance of having a purpose.
- The value of the Strategic Compass.
- Why you shouldn't start with 'why'.
- Why you must put purpose over profit.

Life at a STANDSTILL

Adrian didn't start Treadmill with any grand ambitions to change the world. Nor did he set out with a burning desire to make lots of money. In the beginning, he just wanted to make a living doing what he enjoyed and provide for his family.

As Treadmill has grown though, things have changed. Adrian has enjoyed some of the fruits of his hard work. He has become more money motivated. His success has fuelled his desire for more success. He's even started thinking about whether he could sell Treadmill and enjoy a big payday.

Ambition is a good thing but chasing pound signs alone is draining for most people. Adrian doesn't enjoy what he does as much anymore. His vision for the business has become more complex and clouded. This is a problem for Adrian, but it's also a problem for his team and his clients.

Adrian needs a team around him to run Treadmill and they're not motivated by making money for him. Some of them are not motivated by making money at all. Moreover, whilst Adrian needs to engage his people, he also needs to engage his clients. They're never going to be attracted to Treadmill because of the size of its balance sheet. Clients want to work with successful agencies who are on a mission to achieve something both for them, and for themselves.

If Adrian is to make Treadmill into a STANDOUT agency, it must have a purpose beyond just making him money. They need a powerful narrative to demonstrate they're trying to make a difference.

Standing for Something

Your mindset is vital to building a STANDOUT agency, but it's just the start. You can't build an extraordinary business on your own. You'll need the support of a great team and the ability to engage clients, suppliers and partners along the way.

Regardless of whether you want to build a Lifestyle or a Growth business, you'll need to get the best from other people. STANDOUT agencies do this by standing for something. They have clear goals and a purpose that others can not only understand but also buy into and feel part of.

As a business owner, financial goals will motivate you, but you must bring your people with you on your journey.

You need to engage, motivate and inspire the people around you. Financial goals alone don't do this. You need an objective and an agency that has a purpose beyond making money. Your objective can't just be numbers on a spreadsheet.

Employee engagement will be harder to achieve in the future, as businesses adopt more flexible working, it will be harder to get everybody together with more home and remote working. Engaging people when you can see and speak to them in person is often a challenge. Doing this when your team is not physically in the same space demands a change in thinking and a different way of communicating.

In the previous chapter I highlighted the importance of clarity and understanding where you are going. This chapter is about the next stage. Cascading and communicating what is driving you into something that can light the fire of the people working with you.

Firm Foundations

As you'll see later in the book in Chapter 12, I'm a big believer in creating plans. I'm an even bigger fan of measuring progress against them. Yet a plan is a set of tactics. They help people understand what they need to do and what progress they're making. But they don't motivate or inspire people. What you need before a plan is a strategy.

Once you have a strategy it must be ingrained in the business and become part of its DNA. Your strategy can't belong to you alone, it must be adopted by the agency as a whole. To do this you need to use what I call the Strategic Compass.

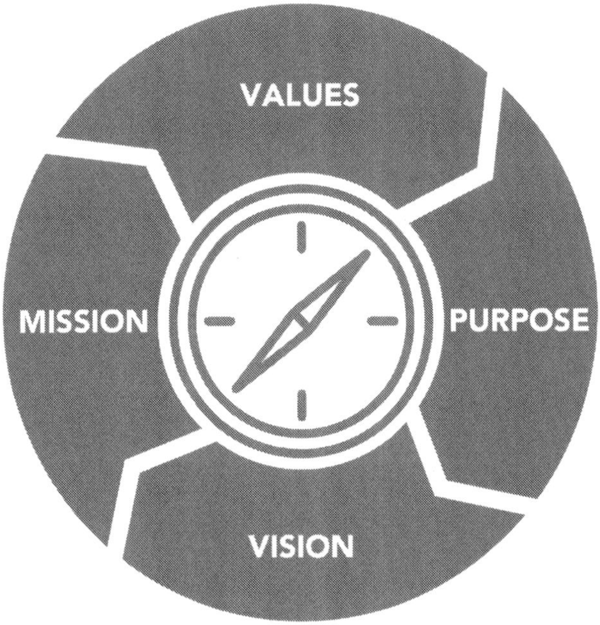

The Strategic Compass

The Strategic Compass keeps everyone in the agency focused on where the business is going and what it is trying to achieve. It doesn't point in one direction; it gives you four anchor points to support you as you grow your agency.

To some of you, the Compass may feel like the territory of big companies. Mission statements can carry a bit of a stigma these days and be seen as too corporate in approach. In reality, firms of all sizes can, and should, use the Strategic Compass. It's particularly important to service sector people businesses like agencies.

All four elements of the Compass are a huge influence on the culture of the business. Culture is a real differentiator for agencies. It can be the reason for winning and losing both people and clients. It is one of the few assets an agency has. A great culture is vital to becoming a great agency.

The Four Elements

The four elements of the Strategic Compass may be familiar to you, but these terms can be confusing. It's rare to find two people that agree completely on their exact definition and application. Some are often used interchangeably. Here's how I define them.

VALUES – What you stand for

Your values are the principles that underpin how you work and what your agency stands for. Your values should guide the decision-making of not only you and your management team, but all your team.

Values are the most commonly used element of the Strategic Compass. They adorn almost every office wall these days, but whilst most agencies *have* them, few agencies *use* them.

People often confuse their values with their beliefs. Our values are what are important to us and what we stand for. They are attributes of what sort of company (or person) we want to be. They are not *what* you care about but *why* you care about something.

STANDSTILL agencies:

- Treat values as a box-ticking exercise. They define them then forget about them.
- Manufacture their values and make them aspirational rather than real.
- Have too many values and/or make them too long-winded so they're difficult to remember.

STANDOUT agencies:

- Define their values based on the values of the agency founders. They don't try to gain consensus from everybody (this dilutes them).
- Have a mix of core and aspirational values (and are clear on which are which).
- Ingrain the values in the business by continually referencing them.

You can express your values in a series of short statements or a list of words. Whichever you choose, have a minimum of three values and no more than six. Keep them simple and easy to remember.

Values are the guidelines that govern the behaviour and attitude of your entire agency. If one of your values is trust, then a new person joining the agency must be able to feel this value in their experience of working for you. An agency with a value of trust, for example, can't be continually checking up on what staff are doing; they must also allow them to make some decisions without management approval. Values need to be defined, but they also must be lived and breathed.

EXERCISE

- List out your personal Values. If you have a business partner(s), get them to do the same.
- Compare your lists. They will not be the same, but hopefully there are some similarities. What Values do you share? Where do you differ?
- Can you combine them comfortably into a list of shared Values?
- Create a list of between three and six agency Values using the shared personal values you have identified.
- Will these resonate with your colleagues and clients?

PURPOSE – Why you do what you do

Purpose is the reason why you're in business and why you do what you do. It gives you, your people, and your clients, the opportunity to form a deeper understanding and connection with your agency. A defined purpose is vital to connecting and motivating your people and is increasingly valuable in winning new clients as it tells a story. It helps you stand out by giving people a reason to believe in you and what you're doing.

The concept of purpose has been popularised by Simon Sinek in his book, *Start with Why*. Yet purpose is still the most misunderstood and hardest element of the Compass to define. Like most things, what is hard to do can often be the most rewarding and worthwhile of exercises.

STANDSTILL agencies:

- Think that their purpose is to make money.
- Or that it is simply to, say, build websites.
- Put off defining their purpose as it's hard to do.

STANDOUT agencies:

- Understand the importance of knowing *why* they're in business.
- Use their purpose to engage people (staff and clients).
- Place their purpose at the heart of their business (and their brand).

Often overlooked in favour of mission or vision, your purpose is equally important. Purpose is why you're here. Why you do what you do. It is your objective and reason for being. It might be the hardest of all the elements to articulate, but that's because it's so fundamental to why you exist.

MY STORY – Frustrated on purpose.

When I was running my agency, I struggled to define our purpose. Frustratingly, it was something that I really wanted to do. I felt like it was a piece of the jigsaw that was missing.

On reflection I made three mistakes:

1. I was very motivated by financial success. At the time, I struggled to see how or why this wasn't a driver for everybody.
2. I viewed purpose as being something that needed to be virtuous. I thought it should be focused on corporate social responsibility, the environment, etc.
3. At the time I wasn't connected with my own purpose. Like values, the agency purpose needs to connect with the founder(s).

EXERCISE

Don't start with why, start with YOU. Think about why YOU set up an agency. There may be a number of reasons including making money, using skills you have acquired, etc.

- What is it about the agency business that attracted you?
- What do you enjoy most about running your agency?
- What frustrates or even annoys you about other agencies (and makes you determined to do things differently)?

VISION – What you want to become

Your vision is your long-term goal and aspiration for the agency. It's what you want your agency to become in the future. Your values create guidelines for how you behave. Your purpose articulates why you exist. Your vision gives you your direction. It's where the agency is trying to go and what the future will look like if you get there.

People in agencies that have a vision, feel part of something big and aspirational. They know what the agency is working toward. Even if they can't yet see it, they're energised and motivated by a bigger goal.

Creating a vision is big-picture aspirational thinking. It's OK if it's stretching and even a little abstract. Many people like to think of the impact they want to leave on the world. If that sounds a little daunting, don't be put off. This type of thinking helps you break out of the STANDSTILL mindset.

A vision is what should inspire people (including you). Your vision is not about the future state of your agency, but about the future impact that you want to have on the lives of your people and your clients.

STANDSTILL agencies:

- Have a vision that is centred around the shareholders, e.g. to sell in so many years.
- Focus their vision around financial objectives.
- Don't communicate their vision to their team, suppliers, clients or the outside world.

STANDOUT agencies:

- Focus their vision on changing people's lives, not achieving company goals.
- Understand that their vision can be big, bold and stretching.
- Are proud of their vision and tell everybody about it.

Let's look at an example:

LinkedIn's vision: 'Create economic opportunity for every member of the global workforce'.

It's not surprising that LinkedIn has a global vision. After all, they're the largest professional network in the world with over 722 million members in more than 200 countries. As an agency you don't have to have ambitions for world domination. What's important is that LinkedIn's vision is to create value for its members. Their vision is not to sell advertisements, charge subscriptions for enhanced user features, or hit sales targets (even though that is what they do)

EXERCISE

Fast forward in your mind to a point in the future ...

You're sitting in your agency, in say, 10 years' time and you've achieved everything you want.

- How would the world around you have changed?*
- How would people's lives be different?
- What difference would you have made to them?

*Think about your clients and employees, not about the world at large. Unless of course you have Elon Musk-like plans for global or even interplanetary domination!

MISSION – How you are going to achieve your vision

Sometimes confused with vision, and often used interchangeably with purpose, your mission is actually how you put your vision into action every day. It translates the vision into the tangible work you do. Or in other words:

- If the vision inspires you, the mission drives you.
- If vision is focused on tomorrow, your mission is about what you do today.
- If your vision is a little abstract, your mission is concrete.

Your mission clarifies who your core clients are and how the agency satisfies their needs. It's how you achieve your vision.

STANDSTILL agencies:

- Think that their mission is a slogan or strapline.
- Use mission and purpose interchangeably.
- See the mission as hitting some sort of target like £X in revenue.

STANDOUT agencies:

- Understand the difference between their mission, vision and purpose.
- Use their mission to explicitly communicate what business they're in.
- Regularly remind their team of their mission and use it as a rallying call if things get tough.

Agency people think they know what they do. They build websites, manage social media campaigns, or code applications to use artificial intelligence (AI) algorithms. These are valuable skills and important tasks clients pay money for. But they're not things that build great agencies. Deep down, nobody really wants a website. What they really want is a shop window for their business, charity, club or society, etc. A shop window that is accessible to the world and is open 24 hours a day.

STANDOUT agencies are not built on digital skills themselves. They're built on what the skills of the agency actually do for the clients they work with. Capturing this in a way that gives your people a greater sense of being part of something is the real benefit of a mission. 'But isn't that the role of the vision?' I hear you ask. Not quite.

Let's use LinkedIn again to illustrate the difference.

LinkedIn's vision: 'Create economic opportunity for every member of the global workforce'.

LinkedIn's mission: 'Connect the world's professionals to make them more productive and successful'.

LinkedIn has a vision that states they want to become a company that impacts the global workforce. Whilst their mission still embraces a global scope, it is more focused and specific. It captures more succinctly what they do (they're connectors) and narrows their focus of who they exist to serve (professional people).

LinkedIn's mission is to connect professional people and make them more productive and successful. By doing this they believe they will create economic opportunity for the global workforce (professionals and non-members alike).

EXERCISE

Think about the vision you've outlined above.

If you have a vision for what you want to become or achieve, how will you do it?

What's your mission?

The power of the Strategic Compass lies in its flexibility. When growing your agency, you will encounter bumps in the road. You will experience significant setbacks as well as major milestones. When the journey is proving difficult, the Compass gives you a foundation to fall back on.

When you need some help making decisions, your values are there to guide you. When your people need some inspiration, you have your purpose to support you. When you lose focus on where you're heading, you have your vision to remind you. And when you find yourself up against it, you have your mission to energise you.

Setting your Compass

There is an order in which you should approach creating your Strategic Compass, but it's not the order that you might think or have been led to believe. Many people try to start with the vision. Others attempt to identify their purpose first. In fact, neither of these are correct. When creating your own Compass, you should always start with your values. Start with what is important to you.

If you ask somebody thinking of booking a holiday about their plans, they'll usually start to tell you about the destinations they're considering. Having a vision of where you want to go is important, but if you think about it, it's not actually the starting point.

The real starting point is your values. Values – what is important to you – dictate the reason why you're going on holiday (your purpose). Your holiday destination is fundamentally influenced by the reason why you're going on holiday in the first place.

Whilst most of us are trying to get away from everyday life and have a break from normality, there are more nuanced and very personal reasons for your holiday too. What sort of holiday *you* enjoy may be different from the type of break I like. Your values play a huge part in this.

Are you trying to relax? Do you value time alone? Do you want to let your hair down and party with friends? Are you looking for a romantic getaway with a partner, or a fun trip with a group of people? Maybe you're looking for plenty of things to keep the children occupied or perhaps a bit of culture and sightseeing? What you value dictates your destination and the purpose of your journey. They're the starting point and massively dictate the destination.

So, you see, just like finding a place to go on holiday, when creating your Strategic Compass for your agency, your values are the starting point, and they form the basis of your purpose. People often confuse mission with purpose, but it is actually values and purpose that are more aligned.

Once you know the reason for your trip, you can start to visualise the destination. What will your dream resort look like? Will it have everything you need and dream of? Has it the potential to be the trip of a lifetime? Or is it an opportunity to get away with the family on a budget? You create a vision in your head before you even start to browse locations and resorts online.

When you know what destination you're heading for, your mind can turn to how you will get there. How will you travel? Who is going with you? What do you need to take with you? You create a mission for how you will achieve your holiday, in the same way you create a mission for how you will achieve your vision for your agency.

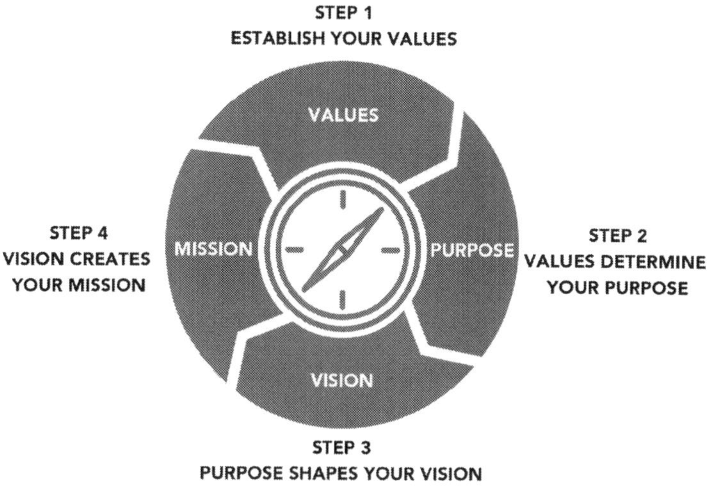

Creating a STANDOUT agency is a journey. It's as important to know why you want to go on the journey as it is to know where you want to go. This is even more important if you want people – both colleagues and clients – to come along with you.

PURPOSE is Pivotal

The four points on the Strategic Compass are of equal value, but purpose is the game-changer for agencies. Agencies powered by purpose stand out because they stand for something. They're driven not by you or financial goals, but by an objective.

Purpose-driven companies not only bring out more passion and commitment from their people and their customers, they're more distinctive. They also deliver financially. The 2018 Global Leadership Forecast stated these companies outperform financial markets by 42%. It also claimed companies without a sense of purpose underperformed by 42%.[8]

It's become something of a trend to 'start with why', but that's not why I believe purpose is so important to STANDOUT agencies. It's because I've discovered my own purpose and I can see the benefits it brings.

8. www.ddiworld.com/research/global-leadership-forecast-2018

MY STORY – Finding my purpose.

When I exited my agency I thought I would leave the agency sector for good. After 25 years, I thought I'd fallen out of love with the industry. On hearing of my exit, a friend made a bold statement: 'You'll start up again, you agency guys always do,' he said.

His prophecy hasn't come true. My passion for the sector did return but I didn't start an agency. I did start a consultancy that works with agencies though. I realised I needed to focus on what I enjoyed about the business. What I liked most was having regular direct contact with clients and working on the agency strategy.

The reason I enjoy these things so much is that they give me personal satisfaction and align with my values. I get a buzz out of growing agencies and helping agency owners grow themselves. I also enjoy learning new things and developing myself. Talking to different agency clients allows me to do this. As much as they benefit from my input, I also learn something from each one of them every time we meet.

My purpose is: To inspire and empower ambitious agency entrepreneurs to discover a new level of performance, so that their agency can stand out and they can grow.

It comes from my values: Independence, Growth, Achievement and Determination.

Finding your PURPOSE

Agencies often find it difficult to discover their purpose. I often wonder if this is because they're so easy to start up. Businesses with high initial investment that take longer to get off the ground go through a prolonged incubation phase. Their founders are not always successful, but they need a tremendous amount of drive and energy to start these types of businesses. They often invest lots of their own money and have to pitch for the financial support of other investors.

To do this they need to really believe in what they're doing. They need to want to create the best coffee, build that new productivity software, or sell houses in a way that nobody else has. They want to fill that gap in the market they've seen that they think nobody else has. In short, they've already uncovered a burning desire that powers their purpose. It's vital fuel that is needed to carry them for a long time before they eventually secure their first paying customer.

If you're struggling to define your purpose, start with your values. They may well be the key that unlocks the secret to why your agency exists and what your true objective is.

What do you want or value most?

There are five common categories that an agency or brand will usually find their purpose is centred on:

1. **To be proud and respected** – To give people confidence, stability, strength or a sense of security, e.g. Mercedes.
2. **To make an impact** – To enhance the lives of others or society as a whole, e.g. Greenpeace.
3. **To explore, discover and grow** – To enhance people's abilities to discover new skills, possibilities and experiences, e.g. Google.
4. **To make people happy** – To give people experiences, create joy and open up possibilities, e.g. Disney.
5. **To connect people** – To enhance the ability for people to connect, relate and engage in meaningful ways, e.g. Facebook.

EXERCISE

List your agency values.

Which one of the five categories above do your values best fit?

Now visit:

https://www.beyond-noise.com/proposition/

Take the agency purpose test to compare your results.

Chapter Summary – OBJECTIVE

STANDSTILL **STANDOUT**

To build a STANDOUT agency you must power your purpose. You need the best people, and you need to get the best out of them. Great people want to work for a business that is driven to make a difference.

STANDOUT agencies stand for something. They use the Strategic Compass to guide them. Nobody is inspired by a goal they achieved, or an award they won, for very long. That bonus cheque is welcomed but is soon spent by most people. The intensity and impact of all these things soon passes.

To set your Compass, you should start with your values, determine your purpose, capture your vision and then create your mission. Purpose is the game-changer. It attracts colleagues, attracts clients and creates a unique culture. Your journey to STANDOUT status doesn't start with the destination, but with the reason why you're on the journey in the first place.

All agencies are in business to make money. But people need an objective that is rooted in values, inspired by a purpose, aiming for a vision and driven by a mission. If you focus on building a great business, the financial rewards will look after themselves.

CHAPTER 6

AUTHORITY

A good agency should offer one service. One thing. Done well. Specialise.

Andrew Wilkinson, MetaLab and Dribbble.

PRINCIPLE #3 AUTHORITY – Sell your Specialism

To become a STANDOUT agency, you need to have the right mindset. You also need to have a Purpose that guides both you and your team. You need something else though. Something that is vital to attracting the right clients and making rapid progress.

The third principle in our R.O.A.D.M.A.P. is AUTHORITY. To become a STANDOUT agency, you must create authority in a specific area. You need to be seen as an expert. To do this you can't offer too much, you must focus. Narrowing your business focus makes it quicker and easier to gain visibility. You need to sell your specialism.

STANDSTILL agencies are generalists. They describe themselves as being full-service. They think offering more services helps them to win clients. They might be good at one or two services, but they can't possibly be exceptional at everything.

STANDOUT agencies are specialists. They're experts that command respect and charge premium prices. They're known for being an authority in their chosen area of digital marketing. They're committed to being the best at what they do, and they're continually learning to improve and develop their skills and knowledge.

In this chapter you're going to learn:

- Why you must stop using the term digital agency.
- The power of expertise.
- Why you must specialise.
- Why building authority is so important.

Life at a STANDSTILL

Adrian's own skills are in web design. He started the business to design websites, but he's expanded what he does over time. He now proudly describes Treadmill as a 'Full Service Digital Agency'. But why did Adrian broaden his offer?

Like most agencies, Treadmill always needs more clients. If they're focused on one service, Adrian is worried that they won't appeal to many people, and focusing on one skill will limit new business opportunities. As a pure web design agency, Adrian knows that Treadmill will not be able to service all his clients' needs and requirements. He might even have to turn work away(!)

Adrian recognises digital marketing is a complex business. Successfully operating and marketing any business online requires a variety of strategies, tools and techniques. He also believes a broader offer is less risky. If one area suffers from reduced demand, Treadmill have other revenue streams to fall back on.

Sadly, like many of us at some point in our lives, Adrian suffers from imposter syndrome. He lacks the confidence needed to promote Treadmill as an authority. He sees other specialist agencies who he thinks are better than Treadmill. He's afraid that becoming a specialist might attract criticism and ridicule.

If he wants Treadmill to stand out Adrian must do two things. He must adopt a narrow focus in a specialist area, but he also must maintain a broad view. Treadmill needs to be an agency that has a reputation for expertise in a certain skill, whilst demonstrating they understand other areas of marketing and how they interact and fit together.

Digital Agencies are Dead

Digital media and technology touch all our lives. All agencies use digital technology in some way. Being a digital agency used to denote something different. Working in digital media separated you from more traditional creative or design-led businesses. You were a specialist.

Despite being around for nearly 20 years, the term digital agency is still in common use. Maybe the label is perpetuated by the industry awards schemes, trade media and agency league tables. It's certainly fuelled by those clients who continue to operate with separate digital and marketing teams. But it's a term that really should have died out years ago.

I want you to stop using the term digital agency to refer to your business. This isn't just because it's outdated, it's because the term is too broad to mean anything. It's a refuge for STANDSTILL agencies. Being a digital agency is not something that differentiates you. It anchors you to a large, commoditised group.

STANDOUT agencies choose to position themselves as specialists in a particular field and are moving away from the generic term digital agency. Many are following their lead. In 2018, 26% of UK agencies described themselves as a digital agency. That number has reduced every year since. In 2020 only 15% of the agencies surveyed referred to themselves as digital (Source: BenchPress 'Under £1M Report 2021'). This is great progress. Clearer differentiation enables agencies to carve out their own niches, stand out from the crowd, charge more for their expertise, and ultimately build more profitable and more valuable agencies.

To be a STANDOUT agency you must specialise. You need to develop deep expertise in a channel or particular aspect of digital marketing and continue to sharpen this knowledge. Being an authority in a specific area gives you credibility, and this gives you power in the market. Being yet another digital agency is no longer good enough. The agencies that will thrive will be those that offer specific skills.

To stand out in this crowded market you need to build authority in a specific skill set and become known and respected for something. Don't be just another digital agency. In fact, don't be a digital agency at all.

The Power of Expertise

Agencies are professional services firms. They provide a service to other businesses in the same way accountants or lawyers do. All these types of businesses trade on the skill and knowledge of their people.

However, unlike lawyers and accountants, a digital agency's clients are not at any point obliged to work with them. There are no points in time where you really need an agency (in the same way you might need a legal firm to help you settle a dispute).

As a profession, marketing doesn't command the same respect as the financial or legal sectors. In some ways that's understandable. You don't have to study for six years to qualify as a marketer in the way you do to be a solicitor. There are no exams to pass, or accreditations you must secure to trade as an agency.

Generally, clients of digital agencies undervalue experience and longevity. If you're a lawyer with 10 years' experience, you're more respected and in demand. If you've worked in digital marketing for 10 years, people are as likely to question whether you're up to date with the latest platforms and techniques as they are to value your experience.

Despite this, whether you're a lawyer, accountant or an agency, your value to a client is in your expertise. The deeper and more relevant your skills, the more attractive you are. Experts are not born, they're made. Experience is a vital component of becoming an expert. Even with a great deal of experience though, nobody will value it if they don't know about it. In a competitive market like the digital sector, people rarely blindly buy expertise. There are too many players in the market. Your expertise must be sold. To sell expertise you must promote yourself as an authority in your chosen area.

There are four ways to build authority.

1. **Demonstrate results** – Quantifying and promoting the great results you achieve for clients is the best way of establishing and building expertise. Nothing builds authority quicker than results.
2. **Awards or recognition** – Awards are overplayed in the agency world (which agency do you know that hasn't won an award?) That said, they do signpost and substantiate your skills and experience. Just don't use awards as the core of your value proposition. Recognition in the form of testimonials from satisfied clients are more powerful symbols of authority. They're particularly impactful when they reference the results you've achieved and not just great service, etc.
3. **Associate yourself with others** – People like to work with people who have worked with well-known names. They think it de-risks their decision. If you can claim to work for a big brand, then the halo effect this bestows upon your agency is often more valuable than the work itself.
4. **Share insights** – If you're only starting out, or don't have awards or big clients, you can still build authority. Tell people what you know. Or share insights from others that will interest your clients or prospects. Whether you're a creator or a curator, thought leadership can turbocharge your reputation as an expert.

The benefits of demonstrating your expertise are boundless. The more expertise you gain, the more confident you become. The more confident you are, the more new clients and opportunities you can uncover.

One-Stop Shops

Most agencies are built on the talent of their founders. They develop their own skills in other agencies or client-side before starting their businesses. Being created in this way, you'd think most agencies would specialise. This is rarely the case. The early years are tough in an agency. Many people take on any work they can find to survive.

Once they become more established, most agencies continue to broaden their offer. Rather than sharpen their specialism, they dilute their strength. STANDOUT agencies resist this temptation. They focus on developing their expertise, not expanding it.

Most STANDSTILL agencies adopt a generalist approach. Why these agencies are prone to broaden their expertise is puzzling. It's little wonder our industry is not treated with the same respect as other professional services. Our sector is in desperate need of more credibility and authority. But how can you build a better reputation as experts when the bulk of the industry claims to be able to do everything?

Agencies usually start out with a set of focused skills, but the desire to broaden their offer seems irresistible. To be seen as full-service appears to be the goal for most. Full-service agencies existed well before the digital age, in actual fact the term was coined more than 100 years ago. Advertising agencies of the day started to plan and book media as well as create advertisements. They realised that the more advertisements they created, the more media space they could sell. There were far fewer channels then; accessing what was available was also much harder. The full-service agency was convenient for clients.

MY STORY – Simpler days, simpler choices.

When I first started out in agencies in the mid-1990s, the digital era was in its infancy. It was harder to access information. If you needed an expert, finding one was often a protracted and difficult task. It usually meant a search of your local area or existing network. The agencies had their little black books containing specialist copywriters, photographers, etc. They effectively charged clients for access to it.

Today, we can access this type of information for free at the touch of a keyboard. We can learn about or create things ourselves online if we have the time or inclination. We can consult with and engage the services of experts from around the globe. Millions of people are available 24/7 to help us solve millions of problems. Lots of them can charge highly competitive rates. Some far lower than we might be able to secure locally.

Before the digital revolution, everything under one roof was a compelling proposition. Now, the benefit of full-service has been eroded by technology. This is particularly true for larger and more sophisticated clients.

Most agencies calling themselves full-service do so to cast the widest net. They're driven by fear of missing out. A belief that limiting themselves to a small number of services will restrict their opportunities. This is a flawed strategy. It's as important to be clear on what you don't offer, as it is to be specific on what you do. This lies at the heart of good business strategy.

With so many channels and complexity, it's impossible for independent agencies to live up to the full-service promise. Thankfully, it seems the fixation is starting to pass. A recent survey of UK agencies revealed that 29% of respondents called themselves digital or full-service (a drop of 11% on the previous year). It seems agencies are starting to want to become more focused.

The survey also revealed more agencies than ever before are reaping the rewards of specialising. Seventy-six percent of agencies under £1 million turnover said they specialise in a particular offering. Of those, 51% generate more than 81% of their revenue from their main specialism.8

The data shows that specialists grow faster and make more profit than generalist agencies.

Despite this, some maintain that you can't deliver effective digital marketing without having every strategy, channel and tactic at your disposal. This view is influenced as much by a lack of understanding of what works for a particular client as it is by a desire to cover all bases. The reality is that breadth of knowledge doesn't make you stand out, in fact, quite the opposite. A range of services doesn't differentiate you now any more than it did in the golden age of advertising.

All Specialists are Not Created Equally

STANDOUT agencies specialise, but they don't all approach it in the same way. To be a specialist doesn't mean you must choose a recognised single discipline such as SEO, web design, or paid advertising. You don't have to align yourself to a social channel and become an expert in say, Instagram ads, either. You can do this, but it's not the only way.

You don't have to choose a discipline. You might decide to combine one or more disciplines to create your own. You could, for example, be a digital agency that builds marketing funnels to drive customers to Shopify websites. You might become an expert in using digital channels to support internal communications in businesses embracing remote working. You might see an opportunity in developing a digital marketing approach for business-to-business outbound lead generation. Or you could develop an app that works as a lead magnet by collecting data from website visitors in a new and innovative way.

These ideas are not channel or discipline specific, but they're not digital buffets either. They bring a set of digital skills together and present them as a solution to a specific problem. The skills can evolve, but by doing so they add to the expertise of the agency. They're not just adding yet more digital dishes to a menu of options.

The secret to becoming an authority is not about choosing, it's about learning. Seeing what works and what doesn't. Spotting patterns and developing your skills. It's about repetition and practice, which in itself is far more scalable than providing more services. STANDOUT agencies don't solve 50 different problems a month, they solve one problem 50 times.

The Benefits of Specialisation

In all walks of life, specialists are more in demand, better paid, and more well respected than generalists. When you have a medical problem you may well visit your GP (General Practitioner) for a diagnosis. They have a broad range of knowledge that can identify a broad range of health problems. Yet, if your problem is not easily diagnosed or is serious, your GP will refer you to a consultant. The more serious the condition, the more likely it is you will need specialist input.

STANDOUT agencies are specialists. They solve big important problems for their clients and get paid more for doing so. They approach the client relationship more as a consultancy than an agency. They have the authority and confidence to do so.

To become a STANDOUT agency, you need to build your business around a specialism. Here are some of the benefits:

- **Premium pricing** – Specialisation enables you to charge more. Your expertise, perceived or otherwise, means your pricing is also less likely to be challenged.
- **Less competition** – Being a specialist ensures you stand out. It's far easier to stand out in a group of 10 specialists than it is in a group of 10,000 generalists.
- **Clarity and confidence** – Being a generalist can be confusing and demotivating. Specialists are clearer and more confident in what they do. They

understand who their customers are, how they can help them and what results they can achieve.

- **Attract better clients** – You become more attractive to the right type of client. Clients that want to engage a digital specialist know what they want. They usually have enough knowledge or information themselves to know what expertise they need. The client is likely to be more sophisticated, have clearer expectations and be able to make quicker decisions.

- **Attract people** – The number one reason to want to work for somebody is to learn from them. This is especially true in the professional services sector. Specialists want to work with specialists. STANDOUT agencies attract a higher calibre of talent. People will want to join them because they know they're committed to their skillset. They will be able to grow in the business. They will learn more. It will not only be a great job, but a great learning experience.

- **Attract partners** – Specialists work in partnership with other agencies better than generalists. They complement rather than compete. This brings commercial benefits, but also can have longer-term implications. Partnerships can be formed that can develop into joint ventures or even mergers.

- **Attract attention** – If you ever want to sell your agency, you'll want to attract interest from buyers. Specialists are more attractive to acquirers than generalists. They command a higher value due to their reputation, goodwill and expertise. They have more potential to integrate with a buyer's existing operation or portfolio.

- **Build trust** – Trust is vital to winning new business in B2B relationships. Developing trust can start from a strange place. Saying 'no' to clients can bring immediate trust, even if it doesn't result in immediate income. I know many agencies who have said 'no' to clients wanting services outside their specialism, only for the same client to return later for their core skills. Saying, 'I'm sorry but we're not the best agency for that type of work' immediately builds trust.
- **Better execution** – Specialisation is not just about perception, it's also about execution. Being a specialist forces you to work harder to define what problems you solve and why you're best suited to solving them. Having a broad offer is an easy way out.
- **Focus scales** – I often hear people saying that their reason for not specialising is that it limits growth. I disagree. You can grow your business in many ways but focus scales better than a broad service provision. If you focus, you can become excellent at one thing. You know how it works, what makes it better and how to do it more efficiently. You can grow revenue, but you can also optimise for profit. Unlike adding new services, you can control your costs better.

MY STORY – Hungry mouths to feed.

I've met hundreds, if not thousands, of agency owners during my career. The majority have been ambitious and focused on growth. Invariably, their strategy has been one of breadth, adding more services to grow revenue.

Adding services can deliver top-line growth, but at what cost? I know many agencies whose revenue, client and people numbers increased, but their profitability remained static or even declined.

Adding services means adding cost. More people means more mouths to feed. Your salary costs increase, and you face more pressure to win work to keep more people busy.

New business is hard enough as it is. As an agency owner, fewer things are more demoralising than needing to find clients that need, say, social media support when your real skill is technical SEO. Particularly if your reason for doing so is to keep your social media department in billable hours.

How to Specialise

Too many people in the digital space are obsessed with the next hot topic or tactic. STANDOUT agencies are obsessive about their craft, not breaking completely new ground.

So how do you choose your specialism? Firstly, a word of warning. We're not trying to uncover something ground-breaking here. With so much competition in the market, it's unlikely you're going to discover a unique set of skills. Neither will you uncover completely untapped demand for specialist services. Don't worry about this; there is a high demand for all types of digital skills.

Your authority sits at the intersection of three factors: Ability, Energy and Necessity. You can use these to help you determine what you should focus on.

Ability – What you are good at.

An obvious choice at first glance, but ability is more nuanced than you might think. So many agency owners are victims of their own success. They're usually bright and capable people. Learning comes easy to them. But because of this, they're easily distracted. They're often found looking at the next new and shiny technology. To become a STANDOUT agency, you have to focus on what you are good at, even what you could become world-class at. This not only means identifying what you're good at but also limiting areas of your operation that fall outside of this.

Energy – What you love doing.

If you're going to build deep authority in an area, you must have a deep passion for it. You not only need to be good at what you do, you must love doing it. You need to be energised by what you do. If you aren't energised, your team won't be. This is where I see a lot of digital agency owners struggle. A passion for something often stems from being good at it, and to be good at something you need to practise. As they grow their agencies, founders often step back from the execution of the work. In doing so, they become detached from something that was once their craft. Digital marketing evolves at such a rapid pace, it's easy to get left behind. They feel their knowledge is slipping and they lose confidence. You must love what you do to become an authority at it. If as an agency owner you don't actually deliver the work, then teach the skills. Become the head of education in your business. There is no better way of fuelling both your knowledge and your passion than teaching a subject.

Necessity – What your clients need.

No amount of ability or energy is useful if you are not building authority for the right reasons. Your clients must not only want but need what you do (ideally frequently). I'm going to cover targeting the right clients in the next chapter, but whatever clients you focus on, it's clearly critical for them to benefit from what you have to offer. What skills are most in demand? Where do you make the biggest impact? What trends are you seeing in the market that you could take advantage of? Choose carefully here. I've seen agency service propositions develop in directions that the founders weren't comfortable with. It's easy to fall into a trap of chasing money, current trends or bowing to the preferences.

EXERCISE

- What is your agency BEST at?
- What do you LOVE doing?
- What do your clients really NEED?

Smaller Focus, Bigger Clients

The goal for many agencies is to work with bigger clients. Working with big businesses has its benefits, but it's often not the utopia people think. Whilst bigger clients offer the opportunity of working on bigger projects with larger budgets, they also come with drawbacks. Working with procurement departments is rarely a pleasurable experience. It's also very easy for a large client to become all-consuming.

Most big organisations have some sort of in-house marketing services function these days. Due to the importance of data and speed, digital work is often brought in-house. The need for a large company to want the services of an SME generalist agency has reduced. If you're a specialist though, you have a chance to get on the roster. Bigger clients often need specialists to support them with specific projects or challenges. Even with in-house capability, there is often a benefit for them to use external knowledge. They need agencies who can provide more capacity and/or test thinking.

If you're a specialist, you can compete for this type of business (and win it). If you're a generalist, it's likely only smaller or less sophisticated clients will want your one-stop shop. They have limited budgets and a limited understanding of what you can do for them.

If you are going to work with a big client as a specialist, it's wise to have a network of complementary experts around you; people you can recommend or subcontract other work to. This not only benefits the client but it's also a great opportunity to form partnerships with other agencies. These relationships can bring operational benefits and even new client opportunities to you.

Getting Beyond Noise

Winning new client business is hard. Cutting through the noise in the market is getting harder. STANDOUT agencies know the best way to do this is to have a clear and simple message.

A simple message beats a complex message every time. You can see this in global politics where simple messages are winning votes. 'Get Brexit Done', 'Make America Great Again' and 'Build Back Better' are the ones that capture attention. NB: You don't have to agree with the message to admire the way the message cuts through the noise(!)

Here's a complex message:

We specialise in SEO, Web Design, Google Ads and Social Media.

How many times have you seen this sort of statement on an agency website? This is an agency that claims to specialise in four things! You can't specialise in four skills. Why would you even want to? This does not build authority or give you credibility. It doesn't make you stand out.

Specialisation is a more focused message. It makes it easier for your agency to build authority. But what happens when you want to expand? What happens when clients ask you to take on more work in different areas? These questions present genuine dilemmas.

There may well be a time and a need for you to expand your services. STANDOUT agencies are not one-trick ponies. They perfect the core proposition first and become a recognised and acknowledged expert. Only then do they explore complementary and interrelated services. They expand their services, but they ensure their specialism remains core to their business and their proposition. Get good at something then diversify or take a tip from McDonald's.

STANDOUT agencies follow what I call the McDonald's principle. McDonald's is the largest restaurant company in the world with over 37,000 restaurants in 120 countries. It excels in the highly competitive fast food sector, a sector it practically created. Whilst McDonalds sells drinks, fries, chicken, wraps, salads and an increasingly varied selection of food, it still specialises and remains world famous for one thing — hamburgers. What's your hamburger?

EXERCISE

- Look at the homepage of your agency's website. Imagine you are a potential client.
- Write down what you would say your agency's specialist skill is from the information on the homepage.
- What would an outsider say you are experts or an authority in?
- Is it single-minded? Is it easy to understand? Does it convey authority?

Good Timing

If there was ever a time for your agency to specialise, it is now. The post-pandemic economy will be difficult. There will be many challenges. There will also be significant opportunities for those that can identify and capitalise on them.

Tough times reveal opportunities for the brave and the focused. There will be bigger opportunities for those that choose to be an authority in a specialist area, over those that try to cover all bases.

I was reminded recently of this old marketing adage: Stick to the knitting. It's a phrase I've not heard for a long while. It's appropriate for these difficult times though. If ever there was a time for sticking to what you're good at, and maximising the opportunities it presents, then that time is now.

Chapter Summary – AUTHORITY

STANDSTILL **STANDOUT**

To build a STANDOUT agency you must sell your specialism. You must become an authority and an expert in a chosen area. This will help you attract the right attention, clients and people. You will have a better reputation, be better paid and be able to be more selective about who you work with.

To define your authority, you need to look at what for you is at the intersection of three factors: ability, energy and necessity. What you're good at, what you love to do and what your clients ***really*** need from you.

STANDSTILL agencies view success as an arms race. They think the more services they amass, the bigger, better and more secure they'll be. STANDOUT agencies don't think like this. They don't build armies; they build special ops teams.

If you can't differentiate your agency based on your core specialism, you have a problem. At best you are a STANDSTILL agency. At worst you are a commodity. Clients have far too many options if they want general agency services. To stand out you need to sell a specialism, not services.

CHAPTER 7

DOMAIN

Identify your niche and dominate it. And when I say dominate, I just mean work harder than anyone else could possibly work at it.

Nate Parker, actor and filmmaker

PRINCIPLE #4 DOMAIN – Choose your Clients

To build a STANDOUT agency you need the right mindset. You must be guided by an objective and you need to build authority in a specialism. You need something else though, something that can turbocharge the effectiveness of both your new business generation and your delivery.

The fourth principle in our R.O.A.D.M.A.P. is DOMAIN. To become a STANDOUT agency, you must establish your domain. You must target and dominate a specific client audience. You need to choose your clients.

STANDSTILL agencies work with anybody. They ignore a fundamental principle of marketing. They don't know who their target audience is. These agencies are happy to work with everybody. They think their digital skills alone are enough to convince clients to work with them. They believe these skills can easily be applied to any business in any sector.

STANDOUT agencies target somebody. They define their target market and dominate it. They're in control of who they work with and why they work with them. They know that having deep knowledge and experience of a specific client domain gives them an edge. They have a distinct advantage over STANDSTILL agencies when looking for new clients; they know who they're looking for!

In this chapter you're going to learn:

- Why you must have a target audience.
- Why variety is not the spice of life.
- How growth leads to breadth.
- How to stand out by niching down.

Life at a STANDSTILL

Like many STANDSTILL agencies, Treadmill doesn't have a target audience. They work with a variety of clients not only from different sectors, but also in both business-to-consumer (B2C) and business-to-business (B2B) markets.

Adrian thinks targeting a niche is harder than keeping your options open. He likes the idea that you can spread your risk by having a diverse client portfolio. He points to the fact that some agencies that suffered most during the COVID-19 pandemic had all their eggs in one basket.

Adrian also thinks that focusing on a particular type of client would be boring. He fears it will limit the agency's growth. He listens to his team who say they want to work on a wide variety of clients. Adrian worries that they, and potential new clients, wouldn't want to work with Treadmill if they focused on a particular domain.

Adrian wants to attract bigger clients and he believes that having varied experience will bring more opportunities. He also worries that these clients might be put off if they see a potential conflict of interest.

If he wants Treadmill to stand out, Adrian is going to have to accept some risk. STANDOUT agencies don't hedge their bets; doing this risks your agency blending into the background. Playing it safe leaves you fighting for clients with thousands of other agencies.

Back to Basics

To become a STANDOUT agency, you not only have to be an expert in your business, you also have to be an expert in your clients' businesses. You can't achieve this if you have a diverse client base. You need to choose your clients and have a target audience.

How would you react if the first thing a new client told you was that they didn't know who their customers were? What if another client told you that their target customers were 'everybody'?

Whatever type of agency you are, these sort of statements would ring alarm bells. Before going any further you would immediately try to clarify the target customers. After all, how could you market the client's business or products if you didn't know who you were trying to communicate with?

Targeting a defined market is not a new concept, it's a cornerstone of marketing strategy. They say that good customer segmentation is worth a thousand strategy meetings. It infuriates me why so many digital agencies operate without a clear idea of which clients they want to work with.

MY STORY – A hard lesson.

I learned the importance of a target market very early in my career. In the first few weeks in my first job as an account handler, I nervously approached the creative team with a client brief. Sadly, it was missing a vital piece of information.

'How do you expect us to communicate something when we don't even know who we're talking to?' came the exasperated cry from the creative director. My brief – a printed copy in those days – came flying across the office.

Never again. As an account handler you committed that cardinal sin only once. The ridicule you endured that first time was enough to last you a lifetime.

EXERCISE

- ▶ Who is your agency's target client?
- ▶ How tightly can you define them?

Anybody and Everybody

STANDSTILL agency owners believe that the bigger the market, the more opportunities they have to sell their services. They're open to working with as many clients in as many different sectors as possible. There seems to be no boundaries or strategy deployed. B2B clients coexist with B2C brands. Logos from diverse industries feature on agency websites. Variety seems to be the spice of life.

I can understand this thinking. As service businesses, agency folk love to think they can help everybody. They're drawn to broaden their client portfolios.

The early years for any agency are tough. Few set out with a client focus. Paid work from any source is hard to turn down. Most agencies are desperate for revenue and so accept any type of client. They operate an open door policy when it comes to new business. Anybody will do.

As the agency grows, some of the initial client relationships grow with it. It's difficult to then move away from these core clients. It's even harder to focus. The problem is that once they're established, STANDSTILL agencies translate anybody into everybody. They believe their early success is due to their diverse client base and that this is also key to their future. They convince themselves they can work in any market for any client.

Somebody ...

STANDOUT agencies understand that the strategy that got them started isn't going to take them forward. They narrow their scope. They understand that anybody and everybody is not good enough. To stand out they need to target somebody.

These agencies not only know who their target audience is, they aim to dominate it. They want to be the experts in a narrow audience. They don't just want to win business from new clients, they want to create their own monopoly by choosing to appeal intensely to a select group of people rather than be mildly interesting to a wide audience. They go deep, not broad, and deploy a strategy often referred to as 'niching'.

In North America, they're fond of saying, 'The riches are in the niches.' (NB: they pronounce niche as nitch.) Targeting and working in a niche can be profitable, but some people dislike the term. They think it implies a lack of ambition. I don't agree, niching is another word for targeting. What you're looking for is an audience you can focus on and own.

Mass marketing is dead and digital marketers, of all people, should know this. In our technology-enabled world, every business can, and must, have a detailed understanding of who and where their customers are. You must target your products and services to a defined subsection of the market.

For service sector firms in particular, the pursuit of multiple clients in multiple sectors is a flawed strategy.

Digital agencies are no different from their clients. They need effective targeting to thrive in a world where accessibility and choice improve every day. STANDOUT agencies use these principles when working for clients and they apply the same thinking to their own businesses. They search for exact match clients, not broad match clients.

The Nerve to Niche

There are nearly six million businesses in the UK alone.[9] You don't need to embrace the world to be a great agency. And you don't need to work with huge numbers of clients. A digital agency only needs around 20 clients to be successful.

Niching does take guts though. Selecting a specific target audience will be a challenge for many of you. You have to show real commitment. You will have to say 'no' to opportunities. Many agency owners agree with a niche strategy, but it's only a minority that embrace it. I often hear people saying they're waiting for the right time. You could argue that a global recession is not a great time to narrow your market. I disagree. There is no better time to go deeper into a market and show how you can help to deliver value to a specialist audience. There is never a right time to niche, so don't wait for one.

The strategy of niching isn't the problem, it's the execution. You must select and commit to a hyper-targeted group of clients. The deeper and narrower you go with niching, the

9. www.merchantsavvy.co.uk/uk-sme-data-stats-charts/#

better. You'll find that just when you think your target market is as specific as it can get, an even more specific niche reveals itself. It can become strangely addictive.

I'm not suggesting you should immediately resign existing relationships here. It's who you're focusing on next I am interested in, not who you're focusing on now. Your niche is your target audience, the people you want to appeal to most, not your current client list.

MY STORY – Three lessons.

I originally joined the agency I acquired to head up their biggest client, a large retailer – I'd worked on several retail accounts at my previous firm. Once we bought the business, we decided to position ourselves as a retail specialist.

Our niche wasn't retail in general, but value retailers. Our audience wasn't the high-ticket luxury brands like Louis Vuitton or Rolex. Our clients were everyday retailers such as ASDA, B&Q, Greggs and Pets at Home. Brands that had frequent visits from their customers and therefore needed to frequently communicate with them. They were High Street chains that needed to sustain and enhance their value perception in competitive sectors such as grocery, home improvement and food on the go.

There are three important lessons here.

1. My own niche experience secured me a job in what became an opportunity of a lifetime.

2. Our value retail focus made it easier to attract, convert and onboard clients. All our clients used us for different things. What they all recognised was that we understood value retail. We knew how these types of retailers worked, how they thought and what challenges they had.

3. Despite having a value retail focus, we often won business from outside our core audience. Niching gave us a focus, but it didn't stop clients in high-end retail, financial services, e-commerce, hospitality, and even airlines, from being interested in our offer. They wanted us to bring some of our retail expertise into their businesses.

Winning and Retaining Niche Clients

Winning new clients is not easy, but it's far easier if you know who your potential clients are. It's even easier if you also know where they are and what problems they have. And it's easier still, if you know what works for them in their sector, and what doesn't!

A narrow target audience makes it easier for STANDOUT agencies to win new clients, not harder. They develop a reputation in the market. They can develop their proposition, messaging, sales process, pitching and proposals to suit their market.

STANDOUT agencies recognise the power specialising in a target market brings to how they find, win and retain clients. It means they don't appeal to everybody. They might even alienate some people (this is a good thing and shows their strategy is working).

Most agencies rely on referrals for new business opportunities. With a refined target audience, the quality of your referrals goes through the roof. They're better, more targeted and often more regular.

Clients work with STANDOUT agencies, not just because they're digital marketing experts, they work with them because they understand their industry. They move from being introduced as an agency who 'does our digital marketing', to 'the experts in digital marketing for our type of business'.

The golden rule of B2B marketing is not to talk about what you do but how what you do can help your client. STANDSTILL agencies without a clear target market talk too much about what they do. They have no other choice. They can't talk directly to a core audience as they don't have one. The default position is to talk about themselves.

If you have a niche it's easier for you to create more focused content. This attracts new and better quality inbound leads. It also opens up other business development channels. You can develop partnerships with other businesses. You can work with firms that do business in your target market but don't do what you do.

Converting opportunities becomes easier with a niche. You have more scope to adopt different payment models. It's easier to explore payment by results if you understand the client's industry and business. You can request the client make adjustments to their business before you agree to results-based remuneration. Your risk is reduced as you have more knowledge and experience. You also have more confidence in what you can and can't achieve on the client's behalf. These are things you can't bring to bear in a portfolio approach.

Whilst winning clients is always a battle, retaining them can be equally challenging. STANDOUT agencies have an advantage here. The knowledge they have about their clients and the sector makes them far 'stickier'. They build stronger relationships with their clients.

All agencies want to be partners rather than suppliers. All agencies want to be able to charge premium rates. If your agency has expertise in your clients' business areas, then the chances of building these types of partnerships increase. Not only that, you can charge more for your specialist knowledge of the sector.

If you're a digital agency 'gun for hire' across any sector, you're a commodity. Commodity pricing is dictated by the market not the supplier. In digital marketing, the oversupply in the market means prices will always be subject to downward pressure.

MY STORY – Legal expert.

A friend of mine runs a digital agency that only works with lawyers. He knows exactly who his audience is and where they hang out. He doesn't attend general networking events or join broad interest groups. He attends legal events and often speaks on the subject of marketing law firms. He's not just a digital marketing expert, he's the lawyer's digital marketing expert.

When a Niche is Not a Niche

I'm always disappointed when agency owners tell me they don't have a target market. But I'm even more disappointed if they claim they have a target market, then proceed to tell me they work with hotels, tech start-ups and chemical engineering companies. This is not a niche strategy.

A niche is a single target, not several; it's not a menu of options. In the previous chapter I said you shouldn't specialise in more than one discipline. You shouldn't target more than one niche either.

Niches are not:

- Types of businesses – groupings like small businesses or e-commerce brands.
- Sectors – broad sections of the economy such as agriculture or manufacturing.
- Industries – businesses working in, say, the automotive industry.

None of these are niches, at least not on their own. A niche must be more specific and more focused to give you the domain knowledge you should be aiming for.

A niche is not professional service firms – that's a sector. A niche is not accountants – that's an industry.

A niche is:

Accountancy firms of up to 30 people who specialise in providing tax advisory services for private high net worth clients based in the UK.

You'll notice something very important about this niche. Naturally, it's far more focused than the others, but there is something more important than that – it's not just about the target client.

The niche describes what business the client is in (accountancy). It segments the market further by indicating what size the business is (up to 30 people). It then describes what it does (tax advisory). Finally, it describes who the client's customers are (private wealth clients in the UK). This is an often overlooked, but vital part of any niching exercise. It not only targets clients by who they are, but by what problems or needs they have and by who they want to target themselves.

I'm guessing our accountancy firm would like more clients. Their clients are high net worth individuals in the UK. Targeting these people through digital marketing is not going to be easy. They will be hard to reach and harder to engage. It will demand different skills and techniques than driving traffic to an e-commerce website selling vitamins or using social media to drive brand engagement for a charity. It needs an agency with experience in B2B lead generation and in targeting higher demographic clients with the right messaging. It's a job for an agency with experience working in this niche, not one with broad experience of many different clients and markets.

The Journey

For most of you the process of niching will be a journey. Unless you're just starting out, or working with a large number of similar clients already, focusing on a niche will be a transition.

Even the decision to focus on an industry feels like a big step for a STANDSTILL agency. It's a step forward in mindset (they're at least thinking about targeting somebody), but it's still too broad to be a niche. This target is not deep enough or defined enough to make a difference to their business. It's a start though, and from this point they can start to focus more.

Whilst most agencies don't go far enough, a few go too far. They approach the process like Victorian adventurers aiming to discover a new Amazonian tribe. They try to uncover a previously untouched group of clients that no other agency works with. This won't happen and usually ends in frustration.

Niches are not discovered, they're defined. The process is more like mining than exploring. First you have to search for an interesting niche. Then you need to dig deep enough that you find a seam rich enough to make a discernible difference to your positioning.

In a recent annual survey of UK agencies, 54% of agencies under £1 million revenue said they specialise in a niche. For firms with revenue more than £1 million this rose to 63%.[10] The bigger the agency you are, the more likely you are to focus on a niche.

Defining a niche is not easy, but some find it easier than others. They might already have experience in a particular group of clients that they can build on. They might have a personal interest or passion, which helps guide the process. If this is you then you have an advantage. If not, don't despair, I have a process to help you.

Creating a Niche

You'll not find or discover your niche. You need to define it. This is a creative process. It's about bringing together ideas and what works best for you. I think of it like creating a meal from scratch. You put together several ingredients that make up your niche rather than pick a ready meal off the shelf. It's the combination of the ingredients and how they are put together that make the niche.

To choose my ingredients for a profitable niche I use the N-I-C-H-E-S model.

10. BenchPress, 2019 Report

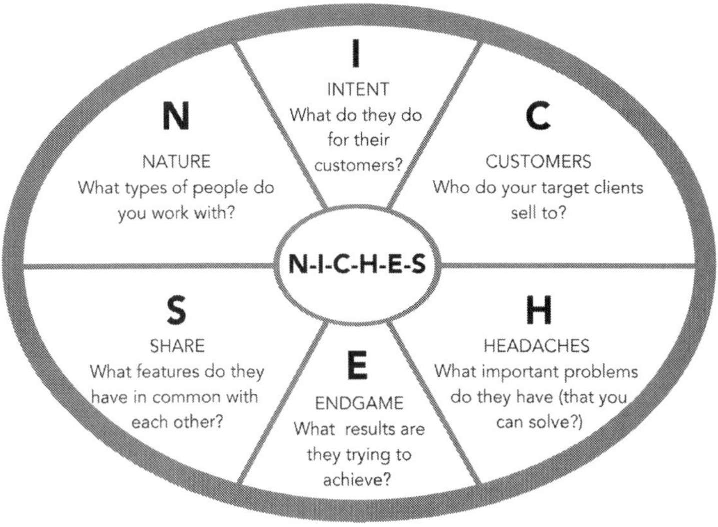

Nature:

Think about types of people rather than the companies or markets in which they operate. What's the nature of people that you want to work with? Ultimately an agency's clients are people. It's a business model built on relationships, and we build relationships with human beings, not companies.

Some examples:

- Entrepreneurs.
- Early adopters of new technology.
- Sophisticated marketers (need high level thinking).
- Unsophisticated marketers (need help to understand and implement the basics).
- People who want you to take their workload and stress away.

- People who want you to make them famous/get them promoted.
- People needing help with digital transformation.

Intent:

Target businesses that share similar characteristics outside of the traditional and broad labels of the sector and industry they operate in. What intent do they have? How do they make money? Think about what they do and what they deliver rather than what industry they belong to.

Some examples:

- Sell a single product.
- Sell a diverse product range.
- Selling luxury products.
- High-ticket items.
- Subscription products.
- Software as a service – SaaS – products.
- Provide experiences.
- Sell professional services.
- Sell consultancy.
- Generate charitable donations.

Customers:

Think about who the customers of your potential clients are. What customers do they work with? Could you work with clients that share the same customers, but who don't necessarily serve them in the same way? People who need to connect with a particular audience, e.g., clients that target an older demographic such as retirement homes and guided holidays? Could you help people connect with a group of customers and become an expert in your clients' customers?

Some examples:

- Customers in a certain geography.
- Customers in a demographic group.
- Customers with a psychographic profile.
- Students.
- Retirees.
- People from minority or ethnic groups.
- High-net-worths.
- Low income families.
- Health conscious people.
- Car, photography or gardening enthusiasts, etc.

Headaches – Target clients with similar problems that you can help them solve. What headaches have they got? Most clients want more sales and/or more customers, but what problems do they have outside of this? These problems could be internal or external issues. The larger, more urgent and more commercially valuable the problem, the better.

Some examples:

- Low sales.
- Low traffic.
- Low conversion.
- Poor customer loyalty.
- Lack of recurring revenue.
- Low basket spend.
- Poor brand perception.
- Low technical skills.
- Limited capacity.
- Lacking specific knowledge.
- Lacking focus and needing cohesive strategy.
- Data not being utilised properly.

Endgame:

Target clients looking for the same outcomes. What endgame do they have? They might offer very different things to different people but they're working toward similar goals, or want similar results. This could be a result for their customers or themselves.

Some examples:

- Improve lives/self-confidence.
- Improve diet/fitness.
- Improve homes.
- Make them look/feel better.
- Better financial results.
- Better security/safety.
- Expand into new markets.
- Open my locations.
- Sell online.
- Simplify their business.
- Automate their business.
- Desire to cross-sell or upsell.

Share:

Target clients in different sectors but with similar distinguishing features. What similar characteristics do they share? Often these can be influenced by where a company is in its lifecycle. Could you work with clients that are cross-sector, but need your help because they have reached a certain point?

Some examples:

- Revenue over £X.
- Plateauing and needing a new impetus.
- New businesses/start-ups.
- Series A/B/C funded.
- New management team.
- Coping with growth.
- Less than/more than, x years old.
- Employing a remote workforce.
- Disruptors in their market.
- Have/don't have a marketing department.

EXERCISE

Spend some time thinking about each of the six ingredients above. Work with your business partner(s) or senior team to brainstorm what are options for your agency in each of the six ingredients.

If you need further help, visit the resources page at www.beyond-noise.com/standout-or-die

A Recipe for Success

Once you have your ingredients you can start to pull together your target audience. You might decide to use four or five of the ingredients rather than all six. This is OK. You don't necessarily need to use the ingredients in the order they're laid out in N-I-C-H-E-S either. Whatever works for you and your agency.

Once you have the ingredients write a summary statement like this:

We work with (NATURE), who need/want to (INTENT) to (CUSTOMERS) in order to (HEADACHES) and (ENDGAME) because (SHARE).

Here's an example:

I worked with an agency recently that has great people, does great work and has some good clients. The problem was, they had such a diverse client base they were struggling to identify how to win more business. Who should they target?

We worked through the N-I-C-H-E-S model together. After a lot of soul-searching and a few false dawns – you'll get these don't worry – we found something. We realised that they had quite a bit of experience and a real passion for working with internal communications departments in large companies. They found these teams easier to work with and more open to ideas than some of their clients in marketing departments. The summary of their niching process looked like this:

Nature	**We work with:**
What types of people?	*People working in big companies responsible for internal comms.*
Intent	**Who need/want to:**
What do they do?	*Communicate company performance, initiatives, news, health and safety and training internally*
Customers	**To:**
Who are they?	*Colleagues / Internal stakeholders.*
Headaches	**In order to:**
What important problems do they have?	*Cut through the noise and barrage of communication their colleagues receive every day.*
Endgame	**And:**
What results are they trying to achieve?	*Change behaviour. Much of what the department wants to do is to get people to do something different and take action. Sadly for many people, because it's internal it's not a priority.*
Share	**Because:**
What features do they share with others?	*These are big companies with hundreds, if not thousands, of staff across multiple sites. During COVID-19, they couldn't run in-person events and meetings and needed to use digital communication more (at a time when the rest of their business was trying to do the same).*

The agency's summary statement became:

We work with internal comms teams, who need to communicate more effectively with their people in order to cut through the noise and get them to take action. Because they're working with a large and ever more distributed audience frequently using digital communication, getting and keeping attention is harder than ever.

Which distilled down even further into:

We are ***external*** *specialists that help big companies communicate big messages with big impact to their* ***internal*** *stakeholders using digital channels.*

Time to Take Control

MY STORY – Out of control.

A year or so ago I was discussing new business with an agency owner, and I asked him how he targeted his potential clients. He said something that had a profound effect on me: 'Oh, I don't get to choose which clients I work with.'

His agency produces high-end WordPress websites. The design and UX of his websites positions his business as a premium offer, and he charges fees that reflect that. He runs a good business, but he gets ALL his new clients from referrals. He does very little marketing himself and has no target market.

He therefore has very limited control of his business. His income is dictated by how many referrals he receives. He doesn't get the opportunity to work on client sectors that he knows, enjoys or feels more competent in. His agency growth has plateaued in recent years, which frustrates him. Yet he cannot drive growth in his business because he's not really in control of it.

Far from being restrictive, targeting a niche is liberating. You get to choose who you work with and who you don't work with. You not only choose to stand out, but you choose to take control. A major reason why most people go into business for themselves in the first place.

Most clients treat their agencies as suppliers. Most agencies aspire to be business partners. To do this you must shift the balance of power in your favour.

Expertise combined with domain knowledge and experience gives your agency power. You can't become a valued partner if you're working for a dog food brand one day and a curtain manufacturer the next. Of course, you can transfer your skills (web design, creativity, PPC advertising, etc.) between clients. But you can't transfer sector knowledge or experience. People think you learn more working with diverse clients. I disagree. You might learn about broader issues, but you miss where the real opportunity and the money is. Deep experience in a niche is what makes you more valuable. You can add more value to your clients' businesses (and charge them for it).

The superior market knowledge of a STANDOUT agency enables them to go the extra mile. They are more in control of the relationship. They aim to dominate the market; they don't let the market dominate them.

With a defined target audience with similar needs, you can also control your own business operations better. You can standardise far more of the work you do. You can optimise your processes, communication methods, proposals, and even some of the solutions you provide. Not everything you do needs to be bespoke and so you can be more efficient, make more money and be more in control. More on this in the next chapter!

Chapter Summary – DOMAIN

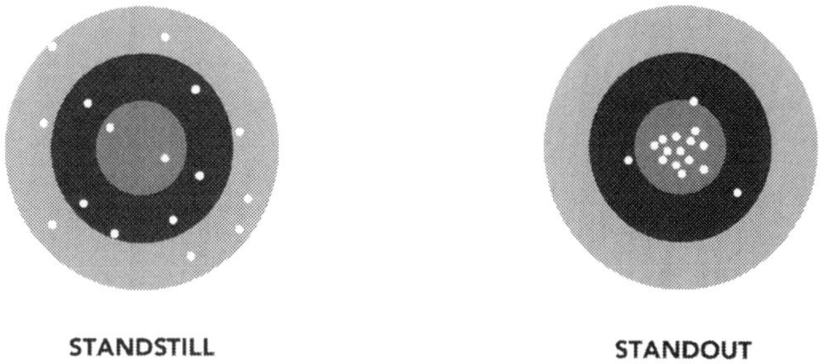

To build a STANDOUT agency you must choose your clients. Defining a target audience or niche gives your agency tremendous power. You can not only attract new clients better but retain them for longer.

Unless your digital marketing skills are unique or way ahead of everybody else's (NB: they're not), you can't build a STANDOUT agency on authority alone. Your skills and services don't actually pay the bills, your clients do. It's clients that deliver revenue. STANDOUT agencies are not only experts, they're experts in their clients' businesses.

Defining your target audience is a critical step. The audience must be specific. It must be a narrow niche not a wide sector or an industry. But it doesn't stop there. Defining a niche is just the beginning. Becoming a STANDOUT agency means you must build deep domain knowledge and aim to dominate it.

CHAPTER 8

METHODOLOGY

The best managers manage processes not people.

Sahil Lavingia, Founder and CEO of Gumroad

PRINCIPLE #5 METHODOLOGY – Productise your Processes

To build a STANDOUT agency you need the right mindset. You must be guided by a Purpose that motivates you. You also need a focused specialism targeted at a specific client audience. To achieve STANDOUT status though you need something else.

The fifth principle in our R.O.A.D.M.A.P. is METHODOLOGY. To become a STANDOUT agency you must stop being a service provider. To scale you need to productise your processes.

STANDSTILL agencies sell *what* they do. They offer their skills as services. Services are intangible. They're difficult to sell and difficult to buy. They're also inefficient to deliver profitably as they're often bespoke. STANDSTILL agencies provide services to clients who don't understand or value them. They attract smaller clients with low budgets and high expectations.

STANDOUT agencies sell *how* they do what they do. They don't sell services, they sell productised services. They have a defined methodology, which makes what they do more tangible. They work to a system and ask their clients to do the same. They're clear on what they're going to do, how they're going to do it and what results the client should expect.

In this chapter you're going to learn:

- Why you must scale to be a STANDOUT agency.
- Why you should not confuse scaling with growing.
- The benefits of productisation.
- How to productise your services.

Life at a STANDSTILL

Adrian wants to grow his agency, Treadmill. He eventually wants to take a step back from day-to-day work or even sell up. Unfortunately, Adrian has a service provider mindset. He thinks that offering digital marketing skills to his clients is enough. Sadly, the approach that got him this far won't get him to the next level.

Adrian still says yes to everything. Treadmill starts almost every project from scratch. They often know nothing about the client's sector or challenges. Every client and every project is different, which makes operating and growing the agency very difficult. To grow they need to work in a more standardised way.

Treadmill is inefficient. They often go way over budget and waste so much time and money pitching for business.

Adrian needs a more systemised approach. One that will make business easier to win and projects easier to deliver.

Adrian didn't start the business to become a manager of people. He hasn't worked in another agency, so he has no experience of building teams. He finds recruitment a nightmare. Adrian needs to focus on developing and managing more processes, rather than trying to recruit and manage more and more people.

If Adrian is to make Treadmill into a STANDOUT agency, he must adopt a different strategy. He needs to move from supplying services to providing products and systems.

The Problem with Services

Digital agencies are service businesses. There are many advantages to operating these types of firms. They need little capital investment. They're quick and easy to establish and can be great fun.

Owning an agency can be rewarding, but they're not always easy to manage. Service businesses are very flexible, which can be a blessing, but it's also a curse. Their ability to adapt the business also means agencies are hard to run efficiently. They tend to throw more people and time at a problem rather than address its root cause. This puts profitability under constant pressure.

It's very easy for an agency to change its approach as to how it solves a problem. It's easy for agency owners to take on different types of work (even if they've not done it before). Flexibility means it's common for agencies to get trapped in over-servicing clients. They find themselves always doing bespoke work and responding to every unique request.

When you think about it, clients don't actually want services at all. They want a result or outcome and to get that result they want clarity and certainty. Digital marketing is complex. Wherever you find complexity, you find a lack of clarity and a degree of uncertainty. Most clients aren't clear on what they want or need from their agencies. Many are uncertain about what the work involves and the technical skills it requires. Few are realistic about what agencies should charge or what value they can deliver. In short, the buying process is risky and painful for clients which makes choosing between service providers difficult.

STANDSTILL agencies rely on people more than processes. They tailor what they deliver rather than provide pre-defined solutions. People-based businesses are high maintenance. People are not machines, but an agency's success relies on their capacity, ability and consistent performance. Recruiting, training, managing and motivating people is a never-ending task.

The Difference between Growing and Scaling

It's become common to use the word scale instead of grow these days. This frustrates me. Scaling and growing a business are not the same thing, despite what the agency gurus on Facebook claim. It's relatively easy to grow a digital agency. Scaling one is a different challenge altogether.

For a business to scale, its revenue must be growing at a faster rate than its costs. For agencies who are service providers and reliant on their people, this is a challenge. For every new client they win, they need more people to service them. People are an agency's biggest cost. In a STANDSTILL agency, costs grow at the same rate as revenue (if they're lucky). More clients requires more people, which increases costs. Even if you grow your agency by adding bigger clients and charging higher fees, it needs better, more experienced people, which increases costs.

To grow an agency, you can add more clients, more people and more costs. To scale one, you need to add more efficiency. This is very difficult for a service based business but it's vital to become a STANDOUT agency.

Why Scale?

I noted in Chapter 4 that you don't have to be big to be a STANDOUT agency. You don't have to want to be a large business, or Growth agency, as I call it. Lifestyle agencies can be STANDOUT agencies. But whilst overall growth isn't important, you do have to scale your business. You'll find other benefits from scaling that are more attractive than growth alone. They may help you run a Lifestyle agency better. They will certainly improve your life as an agency owner.

Scaling brings efficiency, which translates into profitability. It also brings the thing agency owners covet the most – control over their business. Even if you don't want to be big, you definitely want to control what you're doing and who you're doing it for.

To scale, you need to do something more than just grow your agency. You need systemise it. This makes it more attractive to clients, a better place to work and simpler and more enjoyable to run.

In Chapter 6 I explained that digital agencies should be specialists not generalists. METHODOLOGY takes this a stage further. No consultant surgeon goes into an operation to 'see how it goes', they have a plan and a process. They know exactly what they're going to do and how they're going to do it.

Serious clients don't want services. They want to know what they're buying, what it's going to do for them and what it's going to cost. They want a clear understanding of the process they're investing in. Once they have this transparency they start to develop trust in their chosen partner. If they don't get these things from your agency, they're more likely to look elsewhere. And let's face it, they have plenty of options.

To grow your agency effectively and efficiently you can't offer bespoke services to every client that you work with. You need a standardised method your clients can buy into. You also need a repeatable process you consistently deliver.

Productise to Scale

There are many ways to grow your agency, but there is only one way to effectively scale it – by productising. When we see the word product, we tend to think of something physical. But products don't have to be physical, they can be services that are sold like products. This is called productisation.

Productising means packaging your service(s) to market and present them to a client as you might do a product. It takes the emphasis away from the service (what you do) and places it on the methodology (how you do it).

There are thousands of agencies selling digital marketing services, but STANDOUT agencies don't compete with them on the same terms. These agencies know that their skills and knowledge are only a means to an end. They don't offer their services and expect people to come and buy them. They package them more like a product than a service. By doing so they make what they do more appealing and easier for clients to buy. They also make their businesses more controllable, efficient and profitable.

Service businesses are high-touch, i.e. they need a great deal of interaction from people. For this reason, they usually work with a low number of repeat customers (or clients as we like to call them). Product businesses, like those selling cloud-based software as a service (SaaS) for example, are low touch. You can sell online without any human interaction at all. They need a high number of customers (or users) but fewer people to operate them.

These types of businesses are easier to scale. They increase revenue without suffering a corresponding increase in costs. Many agency owners aspire to run a product business and they're particularly attracted to SaaS. Some agencies have followed this path and pivoted into a product model by building SaaS software.

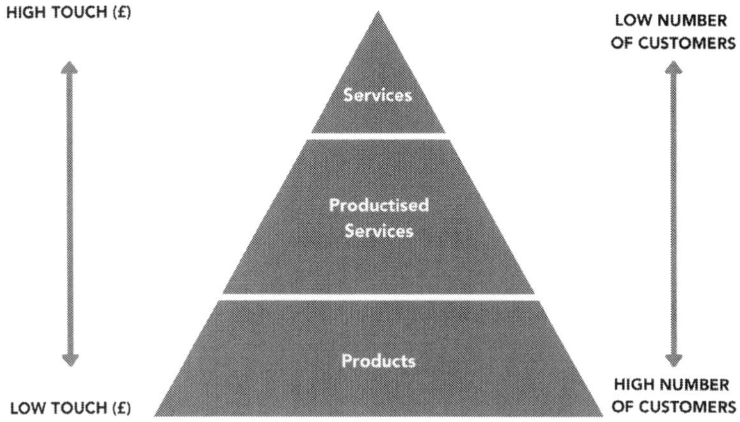

So, we have service businesses and product businesses. Sitting between these two business models is a productised service business. These businesses use systems, technology and processes to deliver their services to more customers in a more structured way. This allows them to control people costs and gives them the ability to scale more than a traditional service business.

MY STORY – A blank sheet of paper.

We were very proud of the systems we had in my agency. Following processes is usually a challenge for a creative business, yet we were brilliant at it. The internal functioning of the business ran like clockwork (most of the time). As you might expect, changing client priorities meant that deadlines were often tight and workload frequently stressful. Despite this, our processes enabled us to deliver a huge volume of work, to demanding deadlines with incredible accuracy. I was frequently in awe of what we achieved. But I was also frustrated.

Whilst we were great at the admin and execution, the creative process itself and the client interface was not structured. Most of our projects started with a completely new brief, a blank flip chart and a lot of head-scratching.

There were positives to this, of course. No day was ever the same. The ideation was a lot of fun. But it's a costly and inefficient way of working. It's not scalable. You're paid on the input (the hours you put in) and measured on the output (the creative work). Both are judged subjectively by your clients.

During my time running the agency, I often yearned to own a product business rather than a creative firm. I thought it would be easier to run. I was wrong. Selling products is no easier than selling services, although the challenges might be different. I know now that I didn't want either a service business or a product business. I wanted a productised service business.

Productising Principles

Unlike a software product, the ingredients for a productised service already exist in your agency. It's a much easier strategy to execute than creating a product business. Most of the development work is already done.

As a service provider, you'll use processes or standard operating procedures (the steps you take to deliver the service). How well structured and documented these are will differ from agency to agency. Productising simply requires you to take your methodologies and processes and put them into a framework; a structure that a client can understand.

Productising your agency is a natural evolution. You can control the process and it doesn't take much investment. You can even productise one part of the business as a trial if you like.

What it does take is a change in mindset. A service business is a 'done for you' (DFY) business – the agency delivers what the client wants and needs and they get paid for it, which is different from a SaaS product business, which is more of a 'do it yourself' (DIY) approach. The SaaS provider develops the tools, and the users use it themselves.

A productised service business sits in the middle. It's a 'done with you' (DWY) business. The agency does much of the work, but the client/agency relationship is more of a partnership.

To reduce the need for high-touch human involvement, the productised agency works in a more formulaic way.

They have a set method that they present to the client and the client agrees to work to that method. The client makes some concessions by doing this. They may not have as much contact with the agency, they may have to do more work themselves, but they also derive some benefits. Clients have a set price and scope and they're not billed by the hour.

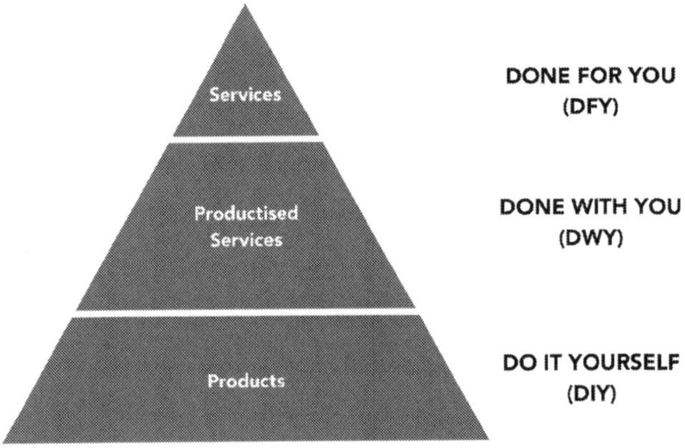

To illustrate these different approaches further, imagine you are going on a journey. To travel to where you want to go, you can drive yourself. This is a DIY option. It's low cost if you have access to a car and can drive. It's great if you have the time to spend at the wheel and know where you are going.

Alternatively, you could opt for somebody to drive you. You could travel by taxi in a DFY option. The taxi driver will go exactly where you want and make as many stops or detours as you like. You can do other things whilst you travel. But this is an expensive option. The longer you spend in the taxi, the more you pay.

A third option is to travel by train; this is more of a DWY approach. You need to choose a set route. You must follow a schedule and pre-book, but you get to the destination faster, and whilst it's not as convenient as being driven, you can do other things during the journey. You also have the option to upgrade by paying a premium for higher end services and more flexibility.

The Benefits

Productising your agency makes it easier for your clients, easier for your people and easier for you.

1. Benefits for your clients/prospective clients

Breaks down barriers – Buying services has more barriers than buying products. You are entering into a relationship and there are a lot of unknowns. When you buy services you have to make more of a leap of faith. Do I trust these people? Do I like them? Do they understand my problem? Can they solve it? A productised offer doesn't eliminate these barriers, but it does reduce them. It makes it easier for the client as there is greater transparency.

Trust – A productised service means a client is more informed about what value they're getting. It clarifies expectations and outcomes. If clients are able to understand your methodology, they can develop more trust in what you're doing for them.

More compelling – A productised service is a predefined solution to a predefined problem. Clients don't want services, they want results. They can see results better with products than they can with services. Agencies can move the conversation away from hours worked to value delivered. Consider a simple example.

A web design agency might say:

We build websites.

A productised web design agency might say:

We create digital shops for traditional independent retailers that want to take their businesses online. For £5,000 we take our clients from Retail to e-tail in just 35 days.

Experience – STANDOUT agencies make sure their new clients benefit from others that have gone before them. If you're starting each new client engagement afresh, the client only benefits from the time you spend on them. If you productise your services, you will refine and improve them over time. Every client benefits from the mistakes you've made and experiences you've had before working with them.

2. Benefits for your people

Simplicity – To productise your business you must systemise it. You must look at all your processes, how they work and how they fit together. This brings greater simplicity, efficiency and better ways of working.

Onboarding – Training new people is easier with a productised agency. It's easier for new recruits to understand and learn. It's easier for your existing people to train and coach new colleagues.

Continuity – One of the biggest advantages of a productised agency is that the processes and information are more visible and secure. You store your business information centrally rather than in one or two people's heads. If key people are unable to work or leave the business, the agency is not left in jeopardy. The operating systems are clear and accessible to everyone.

Innovation – Some think that productising stifles innovation. In my experience, it does the opposite. If you productise you get to refine and improve your method. It helps you improve what you do and generates new ideas. You also free up more time for your people to do other things.

3. Benefits for you and your agency operations

Win clients faster – Digital agencies often have long buying cycles for winning new clients. Productisation enables clients to quickly understand and trust in what you do. The quicker you can get a client to trust you, the faster they will sign up to work with you.

Avoids commoditisation – All agencies want to avoid clients choosing them on price. Digital marketing services have become commoditised. Productisation can help you differentiate your offer from the STANDSTILL service providers.

More profit – By productising you simplify. Less complexity brings greater efficiency. Your need for more people resources reduces, and/or your need for more higher paid staff is reduced. You can free up people to take on more clients or reduce costs and make more profit.

Fewer Pitches – Clients run pitches to help them decide which agency is best suited to them. One of the main reasons for this is the lack of differentiation. Productisation differentiates your agency. You are not offering the same as everybody else.

Less time tracking – Time recording is still the norm for most agencies. Productisation helps you shift the emphasis from hours to deliverables and outcomes (both internally and with clients). The focus moves to getting the work done efficiently rather than recording more hours. The mindset shifts from how many hours you need to put in, to how much you deliver for how many clients.

Higher Pricing – Clients only like to pay for what they can see. If you have a productised offer it's easier for your prospects to evaluate. They'll feel more comfortable paying a premium for something tangible over the generic service promises of your competitors.

Intellectual Property – Productised services become your Intellectual Property (IP). You can use them to market your business, but they can also prove valuable if you decide to sell the agency. IP is an asset that increases the value of an agency. It also makes it more attractive to potential acquirers. You can't sell something you don't own, and you'll never own your people (however good or engaged they currently are). You need to own assets, and IP can be a valuable asset.

How to Productise

Productising will mean making some fundamental changes to how you think and operate. It will also be hard work at first. To productise your agency, follow these steps:

1. **Focus on a core skill** – It's far simpler to productise a skill, e.g. website building rather than a set of skills, or a broader offer.
2. **Focus on a target audience** – It's far easier to build a productised offer for a defined audience. If you have a niche you have a better insight into the problems they have and how your productised service can solve them.
3. **Start from the inside out** – Map the processes that you currently use to deliver the service. You might not see them, or refer to them as processes, but they will be there. Uncover them.
4. **Evaluate the map** – What works well? What doesn't work so well? What is defined and clear? Where is it ambiguous? Where are the gaps?
5. **Plug the gaps** – Where gaps or inefficiency in the process exist, build out and formalise new methods to bridge or eliminate them. Whether you productise your agency or not this is a valuable exercise in itself.
6. **Extend the process** – Consider whether you can add to the process. Does it encompass everything you need to do to perform the service? Have you kept certain actions separate in the past that can now be brought into the single solution?
7. **Optimise** – Review the process. How could it be improved? What steps could you take out? Which steps are unnecessary? How could you make it easier and quicker for your team and/or clients?
8. **Automate** – You will be using technology at points throughout the process. Are you using tech to its

full capability? Or are there too many tech solutions involved? What manual parts of the process could you automate? Could one tech solution manage the entire end-to-end process?

9. **Brand It** – All products must have a name. Your methods are valuable, they're your intellectual property. Naming your productised services gives them legitimacy and helps you take ownership of them. It allows them to be recognised and talked about by your people and your clients.
10. **Document** – You should have plenty of notes if you've followed these steps so far. Capture everything in as much detail as you can. Document it so that other people and new recruits can easily read and understand the process.

These are simple steps, but you will need to include a lot of detail if they're to be useful to you. Don't take shortcuts, or assume things are obvious. A good mindset to have during this process is to approach it like somebody has asked you to buy a franchise of your agency in another city. They need to set everything up from scratch. These steps form the basis of the operating manual you will give to them.

EXERCISE

How well do you know how your agency delivers?

If you were asked to write out an end-to-end process for how you produce client work, could you do this (in detail)?

Exploding some Myths

The act of productisation or working to a set methodology can attract criticism, particularly from people that are not process-minded. Here are some common objections.

A one-size-fits-all approach doesn't work for my clients – This is usually used by people whose agencies are not focused on a target market. Remember: Productisation doesn't have to be a single method. It is a way of communicating one solution, but you might have a number of solutions to offer your clients.

I want to build my own software – This is a choice, but you can use one as a route to the other. You don't have to build software; you can build a productised framework around software that already exists. For example, it's possible for anybody to create their own Facebook ads. But many people lack the time, skill or interest to do this themselves. This is where your productised service comes in. If the client doesn't have the time, the Facebook user interface is too confusing, or results are not what they expect or want; they can bring in the experts to support them. You will learn a massive amount from this approach, which may fuel your own software journey.

Productised businesses don't need expertise or great people – This is not the case. Productised offers still need selling and managing by talented people. You may also decide to offer a bespoke premium service on top of your productised offer. This is where you can deploy your best talent and premium pricing.

I've productised my offer. I offer my clients x hours for this and y hours for that at a price of £z – This is not productising, it's bundling hours together.

Productisation only works for monthly recurring revenue – Your productised offer can be either for MRR (Monthly Recurring Revenue) or a one-off project.

If you productise, you can't customise or charge more for bespoke work – This is not true. You can customise when you want, but you can also now pick and choose who you do this for (not customise for everybody).

Chapter Summary – METHODOLOGY

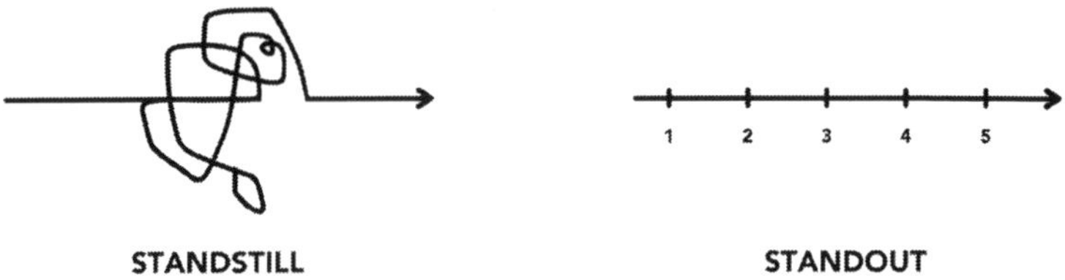

To build a STANDOUT agency you must productise your processes. This makes your offer more tangible and solution focused. Even if you don't want a large agency, you need to grow your revenue at a faster rate than your costs. You need to scale your agency. This means reducing your overall reliance on people.

To achieve this, you need to control the pace and scope of what you do (and who you do it for), which means focusing on a core skill and a defined target audience. Ultimately, you need a business that is more systemised, predictable and easier to run, which means you need to productise.

Productising your agency is the most effective way of releasing yourself from the day-to-day running of the agency, whilst making it more profitable. It allows you to focus on developing the business. It enables your people to spend more time managing systems and processes and less time reacting to client demands and managing relationships.

To productise your agency, you need to move your mindset from selling what you do (your services) to selling how you do it (your methodology). You must devote time to capturing, defining and refining your methodology. Then you must streamline, automate and systemise it.

STANDOUT agencies productise their processes to make things easier for their clients, their people and themselves. They separate themselves from the thousands of other agencies promoting intangible services delivered by the hour.

CHAPTER 9

ADVANTAGE

If you don't have a competitive advantage, don't compete.

Jack Welch, Business Executive

PRINCIPLE #6 ADVANTAGE – Demonstrate your difference

To build a STANDOUT agency you need the right mindset and to be guided by a Purpose. You need a focused specialism targeted at a specific client audience. And you must package your processes to scale. Yet even with these things in place, a vital component is still missing. Perhaps the most important component of all.

The sixth principle in our R.O.A.D.M.A.P. is ADVANTAGE. To become a STANDOUT agency you need a competitive advantage. You must demonstrate your difference.

STANDSTILL agencies obsess about looking and sounding different. They try so hard to be different that they forget the reason why it's actually important. They focus on themselves and their competitors. They make bold claims that they're unique, but they generally look alike, sound alike and blend in.

STANDOUT agencies obsess about making a difference. Their goal is to create value for their clients by doing something their competitors can't (or don't). They define and communicate how they make a difference. This makes them distinctive and gives them a competitive advantage. A reason for clients to choose them over other agencies.

In this chapter you're going to learn:

- Why it's easy to STANDOUT when so many agencies are saying the same things.
- What it means to have a competitive advantage.
- What the STANDOUT Question is (and how to answer it).
- How to craft a Value Proposition.

Life at a STANDSTILL

Adrian thinks his agency is special. To him it is, but to the rest of us it's much like other digital agencies. Treadmill frequently refers to how they're unique and different. In reality, they look and sound very familiar.

Treadmill's website claims they are experts in a broad range of disciplines like SEO, PPC and web design. It states that they're an award-winning digital agency based in Bristol. It proudly boasts they're passionate about delivering results for their clients. Some of these things are true, but the website promotes them as if they're something nobody else can lay claim to.

Amongst these claims are attempts to make the agency seem unique. The people section features Dougal, Adrian's dog. He's an adorable Cockapoo, but he's not the Chief Happiness Officer. He's an attempt at making the agency appear quirky. I love dogs, and I love agencies, but I don't like dogs promoting agencies. Neither do I find the promise of a free cup of coffee particularly compelling when I'm choosing who to help me grow my business online. Have you ever found yourself wandering past a digital agency when you've decided to pop in for a coffee and a biscuit as many try and tempt you to do? Me neither, yet so many agencies seem to think this will entice some new clients through the door.

I don't mean to poke fun at Adrian here, but the reality is that these things have been done so many times before. The truth is, Treadmill doesn't have a clear competitive advantage, and they so desperately need one.

Buzzword Bingo

All digital agency owners know they operate in a competitive market. They also know that to be successful they must stand out. Being distinctive is vital to attracting attention and building awareness for any brand or business. Agencies are no different.

STANDSTILL agencies desperately try to sound unique and interesting, but invariably manage to achieve the opposite. They usually end up sounding the same as each other. They use similar words to describe themselves, which have become 'agency speak' buzzwords.

The real issue here is not that the words are the same, it's more the fact that they're focused on the agency not on the client.

Self-serving – They're statements about the agency, not the client. They're about what the agency thinks and wants rather than what clients need.

Hygiene factors – STANDSTILL agencies promote basic requirements as if they're unique. Why would you ever consider working with somebody who didn't offer you great service? Or an agency that wasn't focused on delivering results for you? You wouldn't, of course, but these agencies claim things like employing great people and being results-focused as if they're an advantage. They're really only table stakes to get into the game.

Comparatives – Common agency messaging tries to differentiate themselves from their competition. They try to use established issues or fears that the client might have to reassure them that these things won't happen with them. In other words, 'We're not like those other guys,' rather than, 'This is what we can do for you.' This is lazy marketing. Don't try to distance yourself from the competition, position yourself closer to your clients.

Platitudes – You don't want to be seen to be using all the same old clichés that other agencies do. Statements such as: 'We have a friendly can-do attitude' are meaningless. At best they can only be judged through experience.

Features – They focus on features rather than benefits. Full service is a feature of the agency. It's not a benefit to the client unless it's expressed as such. Awards are a feature too. The only client that benefited from the award was the one whose work it was for. Even they didn't really gain from the award itself, but from the work it recognised.

MY STORY – Don't wee on yourself!

Sadly, it's a long time since I was at university, but every now and again I still refer to the odd anecdote from those days.

One particular favourite is the morning when my marketing communications lecturer was giving me feedback on an assignment. The brief was to create an advert for an imaginary product we were selling.

'Gareth you're wee-ing all over yourself!' he exclaimed in front of a packed lecture theatre. Immediately grabbing the attention of a room full of largely hungover students. He continued, 'You're talking about yourself all the time. You use the word 'we' far too much. The customer doesn't care about **you**, they care about **themselves.**'

A lesson that stands the test of time. Your clients aren't interested in your agency, they're interested in what your agency can do for them.

Time to Compete

Competitive advantage is what makes a customer choose one business over another. Understanding and promoting their competitive advantage can help companies win more market share. If you don't have an edge over the competition you can't compete. If you can't compete in this market you're as good as dead.

Influential academic and author, Michael Porter, defined three strategies to obtain competitive advantage. Cost leadership (no frills and lowest prices), Differentiation (creating uniquely desirable products and services) and Focus (offering a specialised service in a niche market). He then subdivided Focus into two parts: Cost Focus and Differentiation Focus.

Michael Porter's competitive advantage strategies.

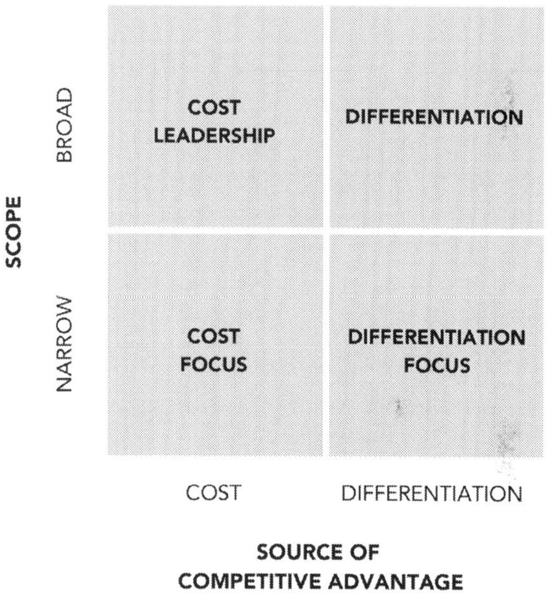

Cost leadership can be achieved by gaining economies of scale and using them to produce high volume at low cost. This is impossible for agencies. The agency business model doesn't create economies of scale. The underlying competitive advantage of all agencies are their people.

Better people cost more, so better agencies will always cost more to run, not less.

If cost leadership is a non-starter, what other options do agencies have? Differentiation is about creating uniquely desirable products and services. Unless they have unique skills, or their own technology, for most agencies this doesn't work either. It just leads to the unsubstantiated, and often imitated, claims we see from most STANDSTILL agencies.

The best agencies choose the third option – they focus. They offer specialised services to a niche market. Porter split the focus strategy into two variants for a reason. Cost Focus exploits differences in cost behaviour in certain segments. Differentiation Focus exploits the special needs of buyers in certain segments. STANDOUT agencies use Differentiation Focus as their competitive advantage. They differentiate themselves within a focused market, exploiting the special needs of clients.

STANDOUT agencies don't try to differentiate themselves from other agencies. They differentiate themselves by focusing on solving the problems and making a difference for their clients. STANDOUT agencies give their clients an advantage. They don't do this by sounding different, but by delivering a difference. They give their clients value that they can't get anywhere else.

The Difference is Value

Nobody cares why you think you're different. They care what difference you can make to their lives. Clients aren't interested in the features of your agency. They're interested in how those features translate into things that benefit and add value to their business.

But what constitutes value for clients? Value can mean different things to different people. All clients want to know what problems you are going to solve for them (or opportunities you are going to help them take advantage of). The bigger the problems your agency solves, the bigger the opportunities you create for yourself. Solving bigger problems allows you to charge bigger fees and make more money. The more value you can create for others, the more value you can create for yourself.

The issue for STANDSTILL agencies is that they try to solve a problem that doesn't exist. They focus on solving the problem of availability. They promote themselves as being available to build websites or supply digital services. They exist to satisfy demand. Unfortunately, their skills are not a scarce commodity. Clients have plenty of options and can source alternatives online from around the world.

STANDOUT agencies identify what problems their clients have or what opportunities they can help them exploit. They market their agency as the solution to their clients' problems. They create demand for their particular set of skills, experience and expertise.

The Standout Question

To create superior value for your clients, you need to deliver superior benefits. Good marketing agencies don't create communication for new clients without first understanding not only what their clients do, but also how what they do benefits their customers. Why do their customers buy from their clients? The first thing we look for is the benefits of what our clients do.

Yet agencies struggle to apply this thinking to our own businesses. They talk about the functional attributes of our business such as the services they provide. These are important, but they're not a reason for clients to hire you over others. They don't make you STANDOUT.

When they're searching for a new agency, most clients talk to more than one firm. Whether they run a formal pitch or meet with a selection of candidates. The process usually ends in similar circumstances.

Most agencies look and sound pretty much the same. This often forces clients to base an important decision on two factors: chemistry and price. If everyone is offering more or less the same thing, rather than try to find the agency with the best capabilities and expertise, they default to focusing on which one they feel they can get on with the best.

If the chemistry is good with more than one agency, then they have to choose between them. Price is a factor that's always important and everybody thinks they understand. Unfortunately, it doesn't make for a reliable way to select the best agencies. STANDOUT agencies are never the cheapest.

This leaves agencies with a big problem. Good chemistry is vital for client agency relationships, but it's too intangible to build your business around. And no agency wants to compete on price.

To avoid this trap, you need to make clients choose you, not because they like the look of you or you fit within their budget, but for a more compelling reason. You need to provide the answer to what I call the STANDOUT Question.

Whether you're in a pitch, a formal meeting, networking or even socialising, the STANDOUT Question can come out of nowhere. It's when somebody asks:

'Why would I work with your agency over somebody else?'

Have you ever been on the receiving end of this question? It really focuses your mind and tests your confidence. Can you answer it confidently and quickly?

EXERCISE

Grab your phone and find the voice recorder app.

Now give yourself about 30 seconds as a time limit and answer the STANDOUT Question:

'Why would I work with your agency over somebody else?'

Listen to the recording playback. How do you feel about your answer?

Is it clear and compelling? Does it give a genuine point of difference over other agencies? Is the reason a tangible client benefit or something that you just like to think is good about your agency?

Is it a STANDSTILL or a STANDOUT answer?

MY STORY – A confession.

I'm going to tell you a secret. It's quite a painful admission for me. It's something I've hidden for many years. For much of my agency career, I wrestled with the same question: What do we actually do?

For agency owners that actually take the time to think about it, this is the stuff of nightmares. I'll admit the answer never came easy to me. I spent a vast amount of time thinking and debating it. It gave me countless headaches. Yet I owned a very successful agency.

People might find it ludicrous that somebody running an established business, of significant size, wasn't actually sure of what they did. They might find it hard to believe I was in marketing.

Before you think I'm completely mad, let me clarify. Of course, I knew what we did. We delivered marketing services for our clients. We created and published thousands of pieces of communication on our clients' behalf every year. We often did it under significant time and cost pressures. We achieved it with creativity and incredible accuracy. It was always delivered with a first-class attitude to client service and satisfaction.

But I was plagued by the fact that the benefits were often lost. We had a broad offer. I didn't feel as if we had the depth of expertise I would have liked. I felt we tried to do too much. It didn't feel sustainable. And I didn't feel we could ever truly communicate what we did better than the other agencies. In short, I didn't articulate our competitive advantage well enough.

Defining your Difference

How do you define your difference and create a competitive advantage? The answer is simple – you create a Value Proposition (VP). A VP is a promise of value to be delivered. It's the reason a client should buy from you. It's the answer to the STANDOUT Question.

There are two stages to creating a VP. First, you need to establish your context (your positioning) and then communicate your contract (the promise of the value you will deliver).

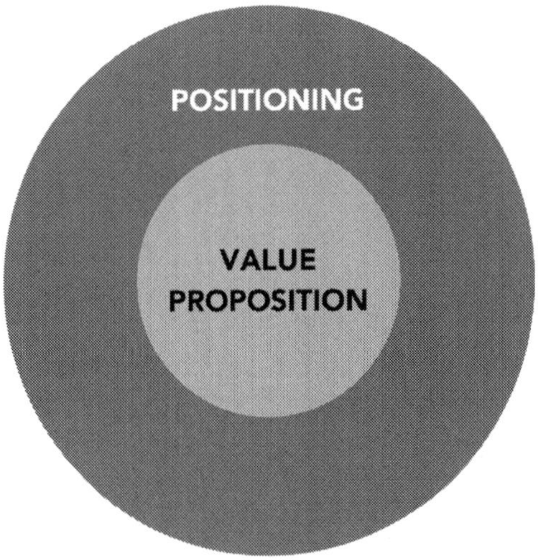

There is immense benefit to be gained from establishing your VP. By doing so you define your agency strategy, differentiate yourself and give yourself a competitive advantage. Both these stages involve strategic choices. Whilst they may well end up being represented in a carefully constructed set of words, the purpose here is not to create statements, taglines or straplines. The purpose is to be able to clearly communicate what you do, who you do it for and what benefit they get from working with you. What value does your client get in exchange for the fees they pay you?

1. CONTEXT – Your Positioning

When considering, buying or working with a new organisation we need a frame of reference. We need some context. Context allows us to decide if we're looking in the right place for something – or somebody – we want. The context is established by successfully positioning your agency.

Positioning is the foundation of your agency strategy and your VP. It is the Focus option in Michael Porter's three competitive advantage strategies. As the name implies, it is the position your agency occupies in the market. It's about you and where your agency sits in the minds of your clients and the people you work with. This is important so I'll repeat it; it's about how ***they*** see you, not how you see yourself.

Poor positioning is the number one reason why STANDSTILL agencies hit a plateau and fail to achieve their goals. This may be because they're poorly positioned, or more usually that they have ignored positioning altogether.

For STANDOUT agencies the golden rule is the tighter and more defined their positioning the better. STANDOUT agencies don't try to appeal to everyone, they try to appeal to someone. This starts with good positioning.

Are you worried about the positioning – or lack of it – in your agency? If you are, don't be. The good news is that if you've taken on board the principles in this book, you've already done some of the hard work in positioning your business.

Your positioning is made up of three things:

a. **EXPLANATION – Who you are.** As a society we like to give ourselves labels. We use these labels as shorthand to help us navigate the world around us. The agency world is no different. We use labels like the generic term, digital agency, or more specific, SEO agency, or web design agency. We use them to help each other quickly understand what type of agency we are. You might be comfortable with using labels like these or you might not like to conform. Whatever your preference, I urge you to choose the most appropriate label for your agency and stick to it. It's a way of helping prospective clients quickly make a decision on whether they're talking to the people they want. It's a navigation tool for your clients, not something you have to get a tattoo of (unless you want to!) If you're unsure of which label to choose, pick from the closest of those listed as categories in your best-fit award scheme. Remember this is to help clients. I'm not a fan of creating your own category of one. You can say you're a human-centred digital transformation agency, or something similarly obscure if you like, but you're making the positioning harder, not easier.

b. **EXPERTISE – What you do.** Your agency capabilities and skills. What you get paid for. In Chapter 6 (AUTHORITY), I urged you to sell your specialism by developing deep expertise and capabilities. You can offer a broad range of digital marketing services across many platforms, but if you want to build a STANDOUT agency, less is more.

c. **EXPERIENCE – Who you do it for.** The type of clients you work for. The people you are designed to work with. In Chapter 7 (DOMAIN) I asked you to choose your clients. To focus on a target audience and appeal to a specific niche. You can say you work with everybody if you wish. But STANDOUT agencies make it obvious who they're for (and who they're not for). It helps clients make a decision and it saves them time and money.

2. CONTRACT – Your Promise

Once you've established your positioning, and people have some context about your agency, if they think you're a good fit they'll want to know more. A VP provides them with something else we all need when making decisions – a promise.

The first stage of your VP gives people **context**, the second stage gives them a **contract**. It promises them that if they agree to work with you, you will do something valuable for them. It's your message to them and conveys what value you deliver.

The promise is not about your agency, and what features you have like how many awards you've won, it's about your clients. What do they get in return for their trust and the money they spend with you? The more powerful your promise is, the more clients will be interested in you.

Your promise is made up of three things:

a. **EXPECTATION – What difference you make.** These are the benefits that your clients can expect to derive from working with you. This sounds obvious, but many STANDSTILL agencies lose sight of this. The features of your agency are largely irrelevant to a client. What they're really interested in is how you can solve their problems or help them exploit their opportunities. This is where the value is. This is the essence of this chapter. It's not about being nice people to work with, or knowing something about AI, this is how your clients look *after* you've worked your magic. Are they able to be more productive? Does their website convert better? Do they have more customers? Do they achieve more sales? What pains or problems do you alleviate or eradicate for your clients? What gains or opportunities will you make happen for them? In order to do this, you need to *understand* your clients' problems and opportunities. STANDOUT agencies have a far better chance of doing this as they have a niche focus.

b. **EXECUTION – How you make the difference.** The way you make a difference for your clients. In Chapter 8 (METHODOLOGY) I asked you to productise your processes. Selling services is selling the invisible. You must make the way you deliver your difference come to life. Do you work in a certain way? Have you got a process that you deploy? Do you charge clients in a different way? STANDOUT agencies make their value more tangible by using transparent processes.

c. **EMOTION – Why you make the difference.** The way you make an emotional connection. In Chapter 5 (OBJECTIVE) I urged you to power your purpose. A commitment to a cause is a far more compelling reason to believe than trotting out overused platitudes. What's your agency Mission? What are you fighting for? What future are you trying to create? STANDOUT agencies make themselves distinctive by *being* passionate about something, not by *saying* they're passionate about something.

To build a STANDOUT agency, you must make a difference for your clients. You might not be able to claim you're unique, but you must be distinctive. You must be able to demonstrate benefits that set you apart from your competitors.

CONTEXT YOUR POSITIONING	**CONTRACT** YOUR PROMISE
EXPLANATION Who you are	**EXPECTATION** What difference you make
EXPERTISE What you do	**EXECUTION** How you make the difference
EXPERIENCE Who you do it for	**EMOTION** Why you make the difference

Solving Problems

What happens if you're still struggling to demonstrate your difference? Unfortunately, this is not uncommon. The problem is often that we are too close to our own businesses. As with many things, what we can see clearly in others, is often hard to see in ourselves.

When people find themselves in this position, they usually make common mistakes. They either look deeper into their agency to try and uncover something they've missed, or they look at what their competitors are doing and try to emulate them. If you're struggling to define your difference, please don't do either of these things. Look to your clients for help.

A competitive advantage isn't manufactured, it's discovered. But it's not discovered by looking inward at your agency or outward at your competitors. Only by developing a thorough understanding of your target clients and the problems they face can you determine what difference you can make for them.

Remember, nobody cares about why you're different. They care about how you can solve their problems, or how you can improve their business quicker than your competitors. If you want to make a difference, not just be seen to be different, you must think, client first.

To define your competitive advantage you need a deep understanding of your clients. You need to understand your clients better than your competitors. STANDOUT agencies have a better chance of doing this as their experience with certain types of clients gives them more insight into what problems they face.

If you don't have this level of understanding of your clients yet, don't worry but please don't guess or make assumptions. There is a simple solution – ask your clients what their problems are!

EXERCISE

Grab a sheet of paper and a pen and list 100 problems your clients have. Yes you read that right, 100 problems!

At first it sounds impossible, but if you give it some time and thought, I bet you'll surpass that number easily.

Remember your clients are people first and businesses second. Include all the problems your clients have as people as a result of their businesses.

Now look at the list and prioritise them. Look for any bigger themes that might occur and cover more than one problem. Which are the most important? Which are the most pressing? Which have the most commercial value to be gained by solving them?

Identify the top three major problems from your list (that you can have influence over).

NB: Problems can also be opportunities. What one client may describe as a problem with conversion on a page of their website, another may describe as a desire to sell more from that particular page.

EXERCISE

Now you have the top three problems, you can identify the benefits of solving them.

What results will they get from solving their issues? How will their business be better? How will their lives be better as individuals? What will be the emotional impact they experience from solving these problems? Will they be less stressed? Less busy? Even busier?

Bringing it All Together

As you now know, differentiating your agency is not about having an agency with a quirky name. Neither is it about having a ping-pong table in your office. STANDOUT agencies have a competitive advantage because they have a powerful VP. Having a differentiated offer is one thing though. Communicating it effectively is another matter.

Your VP should be at the centre of your credentials deck, form the basis of your elevator pitch and feature prominently on your website. There are no set rules on how to express your VP; there are plenty of examples and formats available online. Once you have the building blocks of Context and Contract, it is better to make your own interpretations and treat it as a creative process. You might wish to include some elements and not others. It's imperative though that you demonstrate your difference.

My preferred structure for a VP is as follows:

We are a ... (EXPLANATION – YOUR PREFERRED LABEL)

We ... (EXPERTISE – CHAPTER 6)

We are for ... (EXPERIENCE – CHAPTER 7)

We ... (EXPECTATION – THIS CHAPTER)

By ... (EXECUTION – CHAPTER 8)

Because – (EMOTION – CHAPTER 5)

I like this format because it follows a logical structure, but how you write and express your VP is up to you. You may wish to change the order around and express it in a different way. That's absolutely fine. Once it's written you don't have to slavishly use the header terms such as 'we are for', etc. The key thing is it conveys the value you deliver to your clients in a way that will engage them and can be easily understood and recognised by your team.

Chapter Summary – ADVANTAGE

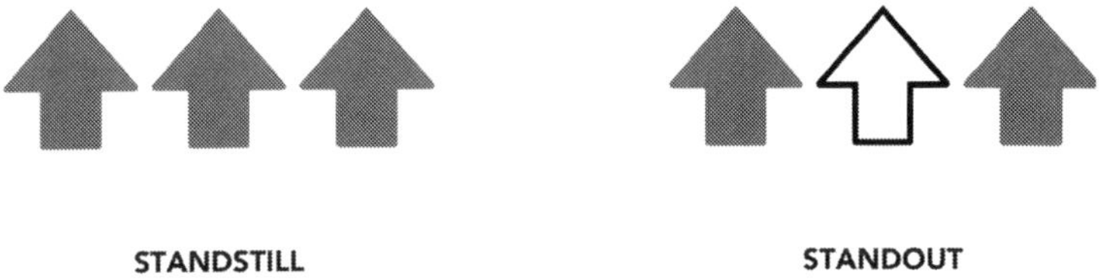

To build a STANDOUT agency, you must demonstrate your difference. You need to have a competitive advantage based on the value you deliver for your clients. You must capture your competitive advantage in a VP.

A VP differentiates you from your competition and takes the clients' decision-making away from price. It gives your agency confidence and a reason to believe in the work you do. More importantly, it gives your clients confidence and a reason to believe in you.

STANDOUT agencies don't just try and look or sound different, they make a difference. They don't make generic claims, they identify important problems their clients' face and solve them.

CHAPTER 10

PROFILE

If you're not a brand, you're a commodity.
Philip Kotler, Marketing Author and Professor

PRINCIPLE #7 PROFILE – Build your Brand

To build a STANDOUT agency you need the right mindset, and you must be guided by a Purpose. You need a focused specialism targeted at a specific client audience. You also need to offer a productised service whilst being able to communicate a clear competitive advantage. But you have one final thing to consider – none of this is of any use if nobody knows about you.

The final principle in our R.O.A.D.M.A.P. is PROFILE. To become a STANDOUT agency you need to market yourself and your agency. You must build your brand.

STANDSTILL agencies are low-profile businesses. They lack confidence. They don't attract people or clients. What marketing they do is usually focused on short-term tactical activity. They focus on finding clients who have an immediate need and are actively looking for an agency. This usually brings them smaller, price-conscious clients who are more demanding.

STANDOUT agencies are high-profile brands. They exude confidence. They know a great reputation attracts great people and a strong brand brings better clients. They invest in marketing to build their brand and their profile. They focus on the long-term benefits of marketing, not just short-term tactics to generate quick leads.

In this chapter you're going to learn:

- Why it's vital to build your agency brand.
- The three brands you need in your agency.
- The importance of KLT.
- The power of your personal brand.

Life at a STANDSTILL

Adrian has a good reputation. People like and trust him. Referrals and repeat business have driven Treadmill's growth. Sadly, this is both a blessing and a curse. It's put Adrian in a comfort zone. It's made him think he doesn't need to work on his own profile or spend time building the Treadmill brand.

Adrian has always gained new business through referrals. He says there's no reason why this should change. But what if it does? Relying on one channel, even one as powerful as word of mouth, is dangerous.

Having no target audience makes building the agency's profile more difficult. The more focused you are in your market, the more cut-through your agency can achieve. But Adrian has a bigger problem. He lacks confidence. He doesn't relish trying to grow Treadmill's profile. Despite his success, he doubts himself.

Adrian claims he's too busy to spend time on marketing Treadmill; this is a convenient excuse. As business owners, we're all busy, but most entrepreneurs don't think they have a choice. They understand they have to market their businesses. Why are agencies different?

Adrian's track record of getting referrals is good, but with more marketing, it could be infinitely better. STANDOUT agencies invest in marketing their own agencies and building their own brands.

Branding for Profile

To be a STANDOUT agency, you must not only build a great business, you must also build your brand. The winner in most markets is rarely the best solution or the best provider, it's the company with the highest profile.

Attracting attention is the very essence of standing out. The higher the profile you have, the more attention you can command. Profile is gained through your investing in your brand and investing in your brand builds your profile.

STANDOUT agencies understand branding is a powerful way of differentiating themselves. They appreciate the important role a brand plays in getting the right people – both clients and talent – to engage with them.

There are many definitions and interpretations of branding. When they hear the word brand, people often default to thinking about brand identity. It's true that a name, an appealing logo and collateral like a website, are important elements of any brand. But the strategy needed to establish, nurture and promote a successful brand is about more than what you look like.

Being physically attractive is a great way of attracting attention. Being mentally attractive is the best way of holding that attention. When it comes to raising your profile, what you say is as important as what you look like.

Branding has been used to differentiate products and businesses for hundreds of years. In some commodity sectors, it's the *only* point of differentiation. The digital agency sector is rapidly becoming commoditised. If you want to create a STANDOUT agency, you have to create a high-profile brand.

Businesses buy Brands

Building a brand and a reputation is vital for attracting people to your agency, but it has other benefits too. The value of a business is more than just the physical assets it owns. Business valuations take intangibles such as goodwill into account too.

Goodwill is what someone is prepared to pay for a business above and beyond the value of its physical assets. These include customer relationships, future earning power and the strength of its brand. A tangible asset is anything that takes on a physical form, such as buildings, machinery and inventory, whereas an intangible asset is a non-physical asset, like goodwill, brand recognition and intellectual property (copyrights, patents, trademarks, etc.)

It's therefore surprising that brand building is not something agency owners seem to focus on. Few invest enough time, money and energy into it. One reason for this might lie in the fact that brand-building is a long-term activity. By nature, agency owners are very reactive and focused on the short-term. They're conditioned to respond to the immediate demands of their clients.

Another influence might be the fact that the work most digital agencies do is centred on short-term tactical activities. Delivering immediate results is the goal when it comes to performance marketing. Quick return on investment (ROI) is what most clients want and what agencies become preoccupied with.

Some people maintain that the real reason behind lack of focus on brand building is that the power of branding is in decline. They claim technology has levelled the playing field, and in time it will eliminate the need for brands altogether. I disagree. Of course, technology is improving how we access products and services every day. Yet branding is even more important now than it's ever been. You only have to look at the likes of Amazon, Airbnb, or comparethemarket.com to realise how powerful branding is. And how important profile is to cutting through in new or competitive markets. When you strip everything else away, many of these technology companies are just brands. They don't produce anything. They facilitate transactions for people. Their power lies in their profile and their brand.

These companies take great care and invest a lot of time and money in building their brands. Some of the biggest spenders on TV advertising – still regarded as the most effective brand-building media – are technology companies. Even Google advertises on TV, in print and deploys out-of-home brand-building campaigns.

Far from branding being in decline, it's more likely that there will be only two types of businesses in the future: brands and commodities. STANDOUT agencies will be defined by the strength of their brand. STANDSTILL agencies will be commoditised service providers trading mainly on price because people *pay* for brands but *bargain* for commodities.

Marketing Blindspots

STANDSTILL agencies aren't good at marketing themselves. They don't have a marketing strategy or a particularly robust marketing plan. Most of the time they don't have a plan at all.

They use a handful of tactical marketing activities to promote themselves. They think short term and don't pay attention to the longer-term benefits a strong brand will have on their agency performance (and its value).

For STANDSTILL agency owners, the cobbler's shoes saying, 'the shoemaker always wears the worst shoes' has never been so apt. They might have a marketing business, but they don't have a marketing mindset.

I'm frequently amazed by the lack of attention marketing their own businesses gets from agency owners. The excuses they make are incredible. They often view branding as purely a design exercise. Or they say they're too busy to spend time on marketing their own business.

To be fair to them though, it's only natural they tend to think short term as many live hand to mouth. Often they're desperate for more revenue. So, they jump straight in with tactics to try and solve what is actually a strategic issue.

I find another problem in play too – agencies don't understand B2B marketing. Many primarily work for clients in B2C markets. They have very limited B2B marketing knowledge (particularly in the service sector). They don't appreciate that it requires a very different approach to the work they do for their clients. As a result, they don't have a profile, they have a STANDSTILL agency.

KLT

Since the turn of the millennium, the way we do business has changed. The power has shifted from the seller to the buyer in almost every market. This is true in the digital agency sector where high demand is still outpaced by supply.

I've already outlined the significant challenges agencies face. STANDOUT agencies need to take advantage of every opportunity they can to get ahead. These agencies provide high-value professional knowledge and services. They don't want to be bought like commodities. They must attract the right clients and people to work with them.

There is a good reason so much agency new business comes from referrals. When it comes to professional services we buy from people we know, like and trust (or KLT as I call it). This is particularly true for agencies.

It's ironic that an industry built on new technology relies so much on word of mouth (one of the oldest marketing channels there is). There are many ways to generate word-of-mouth exposure, but the most enduring is to create a great brand with a high profile.

There's a good reason word-of-mouth recommendations work so well for agencies though. Referrals reduce a client's risk. If a client gets a recommendation from somebody that they KLT, about an agency that they KLT, it reduces risk. Appointing an unknown agency and getting it wrong is embarrassing and damaging for clients and individual careers.

The same principles apply to attracting talent. If an agency can get an introduction to somebody to work for them, the chances of that person being a good fit improves. It's far better to have a recommendation than to be passed a CV from a recruitment agency.

KLT is a form of brand advocacy. Building a profile in your target market is vital to establishing your agency and getting people to know, like and trust you. If you generate brand advocacy you can attract clients and colleagues to come and work with you. Before a client or colleague steps into your agency, they should already feel that agency is for them. The better job the agency does at branding, the less selling/pitching needs to take place. If you want to become a STANDOUT agency, you must harness the power of KLT.

The Multiplier Effect

STANDOUT agencies don't just build a single brand, they build three – different brands that perform three slightly different functions.

1. **Agency brand** – The primary purpose of this brand is to build awareness and enhance the reputation of the agency as a whole. NB: Some agencies operate as groups or have subdivisions with more than one business entity so may have more than one agency brand.

2. **Personal brand** – STANDOUT agencies need standout leaders. A figurehead who is the mouthpiece of the agency and increases visibility and trust in the agency as a whole through their own personal profile.

3. **Product brand(s)** – As we saw in Chapter 8, STANDOUT agencies productise their core services to make them more memorable and easier for clients to understand and buy. The core productised services should always be branded.

Some of the biggest and most successful companies in the world adopt this strategy. Take Apple for example. The business has a strong company brand. Apple is one of the most recognised and valuable brands in the world.

Despite being founded by three people, and now employing over 90,000, one man remains synonymous with Apple – the late Steve Jobs. Jobs played a pivotal role in building and revitalising Apple. His personal profile also had a massive influence over the success of the business and its products. Tim Cook has since stepped into the role of CEO and continues to exercise personal brand influence, albeit in a different style.

Apple is also one of the best examples of product branding. It brands all its products. The iPhone and Mac are amongst the most recognisable product brands in the world. But Apple doesn't stop with products, they also brand their services. The Genius Bar, the Apple store and AppleCare plans are as familiar as their physical products are.

Brands build relationships and connections. Having three brands working for you in the market is vital to building your agency's profile.

EXERCISE

What brands exist within your agency?

Take a moment to list out the three types of brands you need.

- ▶ What is your agency brand(s)?
- ▶ Who is your personal brand?
- ▶ What are your product brands?

Give your agency a mark out of 10 for each type of brand.

- ▶ Where do you need to improve?
- ▶ Where do you need to invest more?
- ▶ What action do you need to prioritise?

Making it Personal

Of the three types of brands, the personal brand is the easiest to make quick progress with. It can also have the biggest impact. When you're competing against similar agencies providing similar services, you need something that others can't replicate. Your personal brand is unique.

The benefits of having a high-profile leader are clear:

- Technology connects us more than ever before. But as human beings, it is far easier for us to build emotional connections with people over businesses.
- Harnessing KLT is critical. These are human characteristics and can be best conveyed through a personal brand. A high-profile leader humanises the agency and makes it more trustworthy.
- Personalisation is a significant trend in our digital world. A personal approach is a foundation for any business that is selling services and professional knowledge.

Even with strong productisation, agency services are rarely bought. They need selling. Personal relationships are vital to this selling process. Even in the digital age, people buy people. In addition to people they know, like and trust, clients want to buy from people who are experts in their field. People they see as authorities in their subject matter.

Thought leadership is necessary to build authority in a market. It's a powerful motivator in B2B marketing. Whilst the whole agency must play its part in projecting the business as a thought leader, it's more powerful when it's driven by the agency founder.

I'm sure that there are other businesses that do as good or even better work than VaynerMedia. But the reason we know of them and not others is because of Gary Vaynerchuck. Like him or loathe him, as a marketer you have to admire Gary Vee. He's built his business through his own profile.

I know a very successful agency that employed people just to promote the personal brand of one of its founders. You may be unlikely to be able to make that type of investment, but it highlights how important the personal brand is.

One of the first signs I see that STANDSTILL agencies are moving in the right direction is when one of the leaders steps up and starts to build their external profile.

MY STORY – Learning from mistakes.

Time for more honesty. When I was an agency owner I didn't do a great job of following my own advice here. I convinced myself that the profile of the agency owner wasn't important. My business partners did the same at the time. 'We let the work do the talking here' was a common phrase in our business. 'It's the team that's important, not the directors,' we would say. I hear similar things from other agency owners now and it makes me cringe.

Only after moving into consultancy did I finally realise just how important the personal brand of an agency owner is. Having an agency 'face' is crucial to developing exposure to, and engagement with, new business prospects.

One ex-agency leader I know built such a profile that his clients were known to take selfies with him after meetings. I've been in the room with him when it's happened. He's now sold his agency for a lot of money. He continues to build his personal brand; in fact, he's become a TV star.

Appearing on TV is not everybody's dream. It's certainly not mine. But appearing regularly where your target clients hang out online or in person is vital if you want to realise the dream of becoming a STANDOUT agency.

Overcoming Obstacles

There are many high-profile digital agency leaders, but building a personal profile doesn't come naturally to everyone. Some people are more comfortable with it than others. There are barriers that you may need to overcome.

Reluctance – Not everybody wants to be the centre of attention. Not everybody wants to become a brand advocate even if it is for their own agency. We don't all want to spend our time on speaking, using social media and other profile-building activities. We don't all want to be like high-profile digital marketer, Neil Patel. Please don't let this put you off. You don't have to be an extrovert to be a business leader. And you don't have to have a big ego to develop a personal brand. Do it your way. Don't jump in, take it slow and build momentum. The more you do, the more comfortable you will become.

Politics – Often building a profile is hampered by there being more than one founder or director. It's usually obvious which person should be the external spokesperson. Unfortunately, internal politics sometimes means that nobody steps up. Don't let that happen. Cut-through is easier with one person as the mouthpiece and focal point. I always like to see one agency leader nominated as the agency figurehead. Even if there are several directors, having one person in this role is powerful.

Attitudes – Flat organisational structures have become the norm these days. As leaders we want to let the team take the spotlight when great work or credit is being given. Those that know me will testify to the fact that I support this. But I also know it can be overplayed. The agency leader should never take full credit, but they should take centre stage. They must accept the applause (on behalf of everybody else) and the profile this brings. This benefits everybody in the long run.

Building a personal brand for the appropriate leader of your agency is one of the most impactful and sustainable business development strategies you can deploy.

If this role is yours, start raising your own profile immediately. If one of your colleagues is more appropriate, they may need to step out of their comfort zone or be given permission. Do everything you can to encourage and support them in making the transition from agency owner to agency advocate.

Sharing the Load

Having one person positioned as the agency advocate is the best way to gain traction with profile. That said, in certain circumstances it might be advisable to split the responsibilities. Every agency has at least two audiences – the market they compete in and the market they sell to. You compete with other agencies, and you sell to your clients. You need to raise your profile in both.

You compete with other agencies not just for clients but for people. A higher profile in the industry means you can attract better people, and in turn, this enables you to attract and win better clients.

Ultimately, success drives profile in the agency sector, but you can influence it too. You must raise your profile amongst your target clients. The objective is to become known and respected as the go-to agency for clients in that space. You can do this by becoming a thought leader. An expert in your chosen area of authority in that market.

You can also become a leading voice in promoting good working practices and being a great employer. You can showcase the work you do in making your agency a great place to work.

It is possible for one person to build their profile in both markets, but it is a lot of work. If you have one director who is more of an operations person or a practitioner of your agency skillset, and another that is more sales or client focused, you might be able to focus one person on the agency sector and another at the client market.

A higher profile amongst both your clients and your peers delivers two things: more inbound enquiries from prospects and more people queuing up to work with you. But the real benefit to this is very simple – you have more choice. As a STANDOUT agency you have more opportunity to choose who you work with, and who works for you. If you get to this position, you'll find it even more exciting and liberating than growing the business. You may even find the added freedom it gives you more satisfying than the financial rewards you might gain.

MY STORY –Targeted profile building.

I was talking to an agency contact of mine recently who was asking how I was doing with my consultancy business. During the conversation he asked who was doing my marketing for me. He was shocked to hear I was doing it all myself. 'But how do you find the time?' he exclaimed. 'I see you everywhere online.'

He was paying me a compliment, but unwittingly he was also highlighting the importance of targeting. The reality is, my profile building is very much a work in progress. I'm not everywhere online by any stretch of the imagination. I just tend to be where *he* is online. There's a massive difference.

Because I'm targeting agency owners, I'm trying to build my profile where they hang out. This is clearly working. It's not down to a secret formula, spending lots of money, or even me being particularly prolific though. It's because my output is targeted at a very specific audience and my content is what they want to engage with.

Quirks and Perks

There's a big advantage to making your brand memorable, and you don't always have to do something big to achieve it. Small gestures with modest investment can help your agency stand out and become known for something.

Twenty years ago, my agency started offering free fruit for staff and a monthly visit from a massage therapist to relieve some of the aches and pains of sitting in front of a computer screen all day. These things are widely used now, but at the time they were unusual and remarked upon by our staff and clients.

More recently, I've noticed an agency generating a lot of social media coverage by operating a weekly book club. They summarise a business book each week and send it out to a mailing list of friends and contacts. A simple idea, but something that people pick up on and remember. Something that makes them stand out.

Another example is an agency I know who has adopted a particularly striking brand colour. Whenever the agency founder attends an event or call he wears, sits in front of, or uses a prop in his brand colour.

There's value in having a quirky attribute to your agency. Something that gives your business some personality and uniqueness. It doesn't always need a lot of money, time or effort either.

Having a memorable aspect to your agency personality is great for your profile. If it's an integral part of the way your agency operates and adds value to your clients then this is the ideal. But it might as easily be something fun like the fact your agency has a band that does live gigs, for example. Whatever it is, rather than it be ever present, try to make it something that happens periodically. That way it can be a regular talking point.

A note of caution here. There is a fine line between quirky and clichéd, so choose carefully. Agencies have a reputation for adopting unusual names and featuring pets as part of the team, etc. I'm not saying you shouldn't do this, but please don't think that this alone will do much for your profile. Some of these things are more likely to make you blend in rather than stand out.

Signals of Success

Building your brand is an ongoing process. Don't fall into the trap of treating it like a project. Your agency profile will never be high enough or your brand strong enough. The market is always evolving and is too competitive for you to ever step back from the process. Once you start to gain some traction though it does get a little easier.

The biggest challenge you are going to face is not starting to build your profile but keeping the momentum going. If you're in a race with no finish line, the easiest way to keep making progress is to set yourself some goals along the way.

There are many ways of measuring profile and brand value, but I like to keep things simple. When it comes to measuring STANDOUT agency profiles I use three signals of success.

1. **People want to work with you** – You're going to want to keep client referrals coming in, but you also need to increase your inbound leads too. Building your profile should start to do this. How you measure your success depends on your starting point. If you have no inbound at the moment then you're going to want to see that change. If you've plenty of inbound leads, but the quality of them is not great, then your

profile should start to attract clients that are more suitable.

2. **People want to work for you** – Recruiting is a challenge for agencies even in a post-pandemic economy. Competition for talent is so fierce that there are always other agencies vying with you for the best talent. STANDOUT agencies attract people. Few things are more satisfying than being able to pick and choose between the best talent. Nothing is more frustrating than making the difficult decision to invest in more headcount, only to find that making it happen is a long, drawn-out process.
3. **People want to associate with you** – Are your people and your clients proud to be linked with your agency? Proud to the point where they're happy to 'wear the badge'? It might seem a little strange as a metric, but people love 'swag'. If your people are happy to wear your agency branded hoodies then you've achieved first base. If they're prepared to buy them, even better. When clients start to request your branded items, you know you're on your way to STANDOUT status.

Chapter Summary – PROFILE

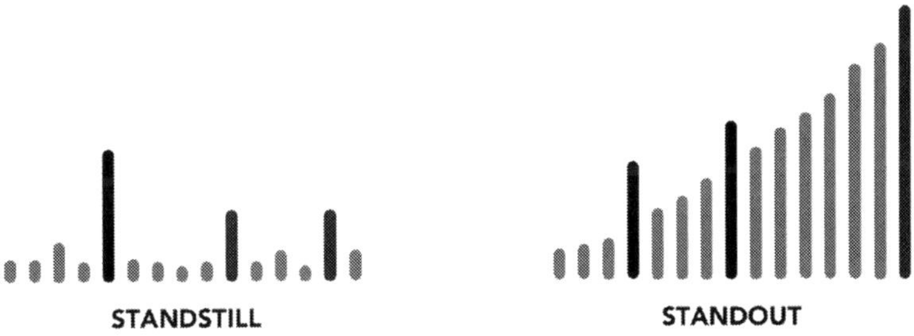

To build a STANDOUT agency you need to build your brand. A high profile is crucial to maximising your ability to attract great people and new clients. Building your agency profile is an ongoing process that will never be finished.

STANDOUT agencies are not just great agencies, they're great brands. Branding is one of the most overlooked aspects of the agency business model. It will not only deliver visibility in the marketplace but actual value to your balance sheet.

If you have all the other principles in the STANDOUT R.O.A.D.M.A.P. in place, you'll already be gaining a profile within the industry, but to really maximise the opportunity you need to focus on managing your brands.

You need three brands to be a STANDOUT agency. Your agency brand, your personal brand and your product brand(s). Your personal brand and profile is a powerful way of promoting your agency and getting people to know, like and trust both you and your business.

STANDOUT agencies build their brands to increase their profile. By doing so they attract attention from clients, talent and – when the time is right – potential acquirers.

PART 3

STANDOUT LEADERSHIP

CHAPTER 11

THE POWER OF FOCUS

Winners focus, losers spray.

Michael Leboeuf, Author

SUPERCHARGE your Way to STANDOUT Status

Now you have the R.O.A.D.M.A.P., you have all the tools to become a STANDOUT agency. Like any tools though, they're not effective unless they're used by people with the right skills. A great team of people is crucial to running a great agency, but what drives and makes a team a success is great leadership.

There are thousands of books on the topic of leadership. The subject alone could fill a book in its own right. In this final section, I'm going to give you three key skills that you need to lead a STANDOUT agency.

These three skills will accelerate your growth and supercharge your progress on the R.O.A.D.M.A.P.

STANDSTILL agency leaders struggle for three reasons:

- They don't concentrate their efforts.
- They don't commit to a plan.
- They don't consistently deliver.

STANDOUT agency leaders use what I call the three agency superpowers:

- The Power of Focus.
- The Power of Planning.
- The Power of Execution.

To get the most out of the STANDOUT agency R.O.A.D.M.A.P. you need to be a STANDOUT agency leader. The next three chapters will show you how.

Life at a STANDSTILL

Adrian finds it hard to give Treadmill his full attention. In actual fact, he finds it hard to give anything his full attention. Adrian has what some call Shiny Object Syndrome. He loves exploring new concepts and looking at new things. He's always coming up with interesting new ideas. It's not a bad thing, but some of our greatest strengths can also be significant weaknesses or blind spots.

Adrian tries to think of new opportunities for Treadmill. He's always looking for the next big thing in tech or which services he might be able to add into the agency. He loves thinking about new products too. He's got a couple of side hustles he's already working on. Adrian likes to keep his options open, which means he's often spending time on things that never go anywhere.

Whilst he thinks of himself as an entrepreneur and a bit of a risk taker, in reality he's actually quite risk averse.

He believes the more options and ideas he has, the better Treadmill will be. In fact, the opposite is true. What both he and the agency needs is more focus. You don't create a STANDOUT agency by trying lots of different things and hedging your bets. You create it with the power of focus.

STANDSTILL agency leaders are too open-minded. They like thinking up new ideas and crave variety and choice. They love to keep their options open. They don't want to pigeonhole themselves or their agency. They fear it might limit them both.

STANDOUT agency leaders are single-minded. They concentrate their energy and efforts. They minimise distractions and narrow their focus. They don't fear being pigeonholed, they fear being unremarkable and invisible. They don't want to blend in.

Expand your Agency by Narrowing your Focus

There's an underlying theme running throughout the seven principles of the R.O.A.D.M.A.P. You may have spotted it already. Every step encourages you to FOCUS.

RESET highlights the importance of focusing your mind. OBJECTIVE unites the business behind a single Purpose. AUTHORITY promotes the power of specific expertise, and so on.

The reason most agencies don't reach their potential is not through lack of effort, it's through lack of focus. More importantly, it's the agency leader's inability to focus that's often the main barrier to growth.

Growing your agency and making it stand out, doesn't come through expanding your field of vision and spinning as many plates as you can. It comes through narrowing your focus and being more single-minded.

STANDOUT agency owners have a different approach to running their businesses. They have a focused offer where they sell specific expertise to a targeted group of people. They have clear goals and a plan of how they're going to achieve them. They constantly measure their performance and optimise their business.

You First

The most important role of any leader is to keep everybody aligned to the vision and direction of the business. To do this effectively you must establish and maintain your own focus. You need to have a vision of what you want and where you personally want to go. You also need to be clear on where you want the business to go to achieve your goals. This is why mindset and purpose are covered in the first two principles in the R.O.A.D.M.A.P.

Even if you are crystal clear on these things at the start, over time your clarity may well become clouded. You will face challenges that test your thinking and resolve. Your people, clients and even other business ideas will all compete for your attention. You may well become distracted, or worse still, become bored and disillusioned. All these things can lead you to search for change and lose your focus.

This is all part of running a business. To create a STANDOUT agency you must resist these diversions.

You must maintain your focus on pushing the agency forward. Only by focusing yourself can you focus and direct other people.

The Secret of Growth

I'm often asked what the best growth strategy is for agencies. People are usually surprised by my response. The best growth strategy is to decide what not to do. Yes you read that right. In other words, the key to growth is focus.

You may find this a challenging concept. It's encapsulated in the quote at the start of this chapter. I remember an ex-client of mine, Allan Leighton, often used the mantra, 'Winner's focus, losers spray', when he was CEO of UK supermarket chain ASDA. Leighton leveraged this principle to guide the recovery and growth of the business and deployed it everywhere. From deciding the business strategy, through to coaching the performance of individual colleagues, focus was the game-changer for ASDA.

In competitive markets, whether that's grocery retailing or digital marketing services, if you want to grow, your natural reaction is to try and broaden your offer. You try to expand your capabilities and/or your customer base. You can be fooled into trying to appeal to as many people as possible for as many reasons as possible. In turbulent times, and these are certainly turbulent times, the pull to adopt this approach can be even stronger.

I understand this thinking, and the financial pressures that often fuel it, but it's a flawed strategy. It's focus that attracts opportunities for agencies (not breadth). And it's focus that scales agencies (not increasing cost by adding people, services and complexity). If you want to stand out, develop a focused offer for a focused audience. Resist the temptation to deviate from this strategy. You will reap the rewards.

Limit your Options

Resisting temptation can be difficult. As business owners, you have an amount of freedom that salaried employees don't. As an entrepreneur you can control your destiny far more than you can when you're working for somebody else. This is a major benefit of running your own agency.

The choices you have can be liberating, but they can also be strangely debilitating. As an agency owner put it to me recently when talking about business strategy: 'My biggest problem is that I have too many ideas'.

What stands in the way of productivity and progress is often not a lack of options, but lack of focus. Often referred to as the paradox of choice. The more choices we have, the harder we find it to make a choice. The harder it is to make a choice, the less choices we want.

Whatever the psychology at play, your opportunity is to try and make fewer choices. It's counter-intuitive, but to grow the business you need to be more selective about what you do and who you do it for. Only then can you start to charge more and systemise what you do to be able to scale and become more profitable.

Agency owners seem particularly prone to temptation and choice. Perhaps it's because owners of marketing agencies are often creative people? Maybe it's because, as service providers, they can easily pivot their business models? Whatever the reason, having options brings challenges.

STANDOUT agency leaders resist the temptation – and often their entrepreneurial nature – to look at every opportunity that comes their way. They use their focus as a protective moat.

This thinking doesn't limit you, it protects you. Your focus shields you from distractions and allows you to get more done. It enables you to make quicker decisions and more progress.

Finding Focus

When I meet agency owners for the first time, they often tell me how busy they are. 'If only I had more time,' is a familiar comment. The life of an agency owner is busy and demanding. You get pulled in all kinds of different directions. It's no wonder people struggle to find the time to do everything required of them.

The issue isn't time though. We all have the same amount of time. The issue is prioritisation. Focusing on the things that are important. You'll never have enough time to do everything you need to do. What matters is making sure you focus on doing the stuff that you need to prioritise to move your business forward.

Most agency owners rush around doing lots of things, but the majority of the tasks are urgent but not that important. Your focus should not be on the most urgent task in hand, or whether you have the time. You need to think about whether the task is the most valuable use of your time.

A simple tool to help you prioritise is the Eisenhower Matrix. Developed by the 1960's American President.

The Eisenhower Matrix

	URGENT	NOT URGENT
IMPORTANT	**FOCUS NOW** Tasks with clear deadlines and consequences for not taking IMMEDIATE action.	**FOCUS SOON** Tasks that will bring you closer to your goals. Set a DEADLINE so you can't procrastinate.
NOT IMOPORTANT	**DELEGATE** Tasks that need to be done but don't require YOUR skills.	**DROP** Tasks that are DISTRACTIONS and/or unproductive.

The key to running a STANDOUT agency is not trying to do everything. You don't need to react to, or even remember, everything. Let the less important and nonurgent things pass over you. Seek out the important tasks and prioritise which of these are the most urgent. The rest should be delegated or dropped completely. It's hard to do, but try saying 'no' more than you say 'yes'.

MY STORY – The Yes Curve.

I've learned as much about running agencies since I exited my own business as I did in the previous 10 years. Not owning an agency has enabled me to speak openly with other business owners in a way I couldn't before. I've worked with people from start-ups to large established agencies and others in between. All have taught me something. I hope I've given them value in return.

When you speak to a lot of people doing similar things patterns emerge. These patterns accelerate your learning. One example is something I call the Yes Curve. It illustrates the period when agencies are in their formative years and say yes to anything. They want to make their business a success and they need money, so they say yes to all opportunities. They offer more services. If somebody asks for something they say yes first and figure out how to do it later.

I understand this approach. It's usually unavoidable and necessary. But here's the thing; the Yes Curve is not scalable. You quickly reach capacity with your existing people. You can add more people to support you, but this doesn't make you more profitable. Increasing revenue is usually followed by corresponding increases in costs. You might grow to bigger revenue but your profit plateaus.

If you keep following the Yes Curve, you'll end up making similar money but have a whole lot more stress. Sooner or later, you need to flatten the curve and say no more. Sooner or later, you need to focus.

Many Hats

Running an agency is full of distractions. You'll inevitably need to spread your time, and yourself, around. Tools like the Eisenhower Matrix can help your approach, but ultimately it's down to you to find a balance that works.

That balance is a sweet spot at the intersection of spending enough time working *in* the business and spending time *on* the business. Working in the business is working with your team and clients on the day-to-day operational stuff. Working on the business is taking a more strategic view and focusing on business planning, generating ideas on how to develop particular areas, networking, etc.

Nobody can tell you where your sweet spot is. It depends on your own individual agency and circumstances. It changes from week to week. I can give you some guidance on where you might find your balance though. You need to wear many hats when you're leading an agency; three of the most common are:

1. **Delivery Driver** – Working ***in*** the business this leader is focused on the delivery of the work. They're either doing the work themselves or managing closely the people that do.

   Pros:

   - Often it is the only way in the early days.
   - You are very close to the work and can control the quality.
   - You remain involved with the technical aspects of the work and what is going on in the industry.

Cons:

- Can become a comfort zone, which is hard to break out of.
- Stressful and not particularly satisfying.
- Finding the headspace to work on developing the business is a challenge.

2. **Firefighter** – Still ***in*** the business, this leader is not doing the work but is heavily involved when a problem occurs. They might have made a step up from delivery, but they're still pivotal to the operations of the agency and day-to-day running of the business.

   Pros:

   - Close to the work and the clients.
   - Making sure things get done and people are happy.
   - Solving problems and sharing knowledge can be a satisfying ego boost.

   Cons:

   - You can become addicted to the buzz of fire-fighting without realising it.
   - You can find yourself waiting for the next fire rather than doing other more proactive things and working on your business.
   - Sometimes the issue is that these leaders are not really needed. They just struggle to delegate for fear of losing control.

3. **Pilot** – This leader spends more of their time working *on* the business. Their team can manage the day-to-day. They can focus on strategy and driving the business forward, or pursuing other opportunities.

   Pros:

   - Great position to be in when the team can handle the operations.
   - Used wisely, your time can be spent developing the agency.
   - Allows you to think more clearly and more strategically.

   Cons:

   - Only possible for a more mature agency. There is danger in trying to step up into this role too quickly.
   - You can easily become detached from the client relationships.
   - Beware of going on autopilot. Problems can occur and fester if left unchecked.

For most agency owners, the sweet spot is somewhere in the middle of these roles. It isn't fixed and will move around depending on the progression of your agency and the needs of the business at any particular point.

As your agency grows, it's only natural for you as the leader to step away from the delivery of the work. There's plenty more to do. If you don't do this, you'll become a bottleneck. You'll find yourself working for the people you employ to support you. If you're finding it hard to do this, then ask yourself whether it's physically impossible at the moment (or whether you may just be in a comfort zone).

Once you're able to release yourself from the delivery, your next stage is probably to adopt the firefighter role. This is a good progression, but not everyone enjoys managing and handling the problems of others doing the work. Whilst you might not want to step back into delivery, make sure you don't lose touch with the challenges your team are facing. You can't help them solve problems if you are removed from what is really happening.

When you have somebody you can rely on to manage the operational side and solve problems for you, this is when you can spend more time as a pilot. When you get to this position, you're at a pivotal point. It's actually quite a dangerous time. Your role as a pilot can be spent guiding the future development of the agency, or you can get distracted. You can be tempted to use this time on other things. If you want to build a STANDOUT agency you need to keep your focus on your business at this point. It's an opportunity to focus more, not less.

EXERCISE

You're probably performing all three of the roles described here to some extent. Do you know where your focus is though? Do you know where you spend most of your time?

Chances are that as an agency owner you don't complete timesheets anymore (even if your team does). Try completing them on a daily basis for a couple of weeks. It's not as painful as you might think. And you might be surprised what a summary of the hours and activities you personally complete during a week reveals. I guarantee you will learn something and have some actions you can take.

Chapter Summary – THE POWER OF FOCUS

STANDSTILL **STANDOUT**

Focus is one of the three superpowers of an agency owner. As an entrepreneur it might not be something that comes naturally to you, but if you want to build a STANDOUT agency you must focus.

Focusing your mind, your team and your agency offer makes your business simpler, more attractive and less stressful to run. Narrowing down your choices helps you make decisions easier and faster.

Focus is as much about choosing what not to do and saying no. The more you try and do, the more complex your business becomes. Complexity is the enemy of growth. Focus reduces complexity and makes it easier for you to scale your agency.

CHAPTER 12

THE POWER OF PLANNING

When you have a map you can start to explore.

Dr Jon Finn, transformational leadership expert

Life at a STANDSTILL

Adrian has always had big plans for Treadmill, but the business hasn't yet reached its potential. He thinks the way to grow an agency is to do things differently. This isn't always the case. The way to grow an agency is to do things, rather than spend time thinking about doing things differently. Decide what you're going to do and put your ideas into action.

Adrian tries hard to grow his agency, but he frequently changes his mind and approach. It's little wonder he often feels as if he's making two steps forward and one step back. Adrian needs to give himself, and his team, more clarity on where Treadmill is going and what the priorities are. What he needs is a plan to guide him and keep him and the team on the right track.

Adrian avoids making plans as he thinks they're a waste of time and lack flexibility. Deep down, he lacks the confidence to commit. Having the ability to change his mind makes him feel like he is in more control of his business. Committing to a plan makes Adrian feel like he is giving away some of that control. In reality, having a plan will give him more freedom, not less. You don't create a STANDOUT agency by seeing how things go. You need commitment. You need the power of planning.

STANDSTILL agency leaders are dreamers. They're ambitious. They have a vision for their agency, and they know what they want to achieve. Their focus is on quick wins and short-term results. They avoid making plans as they think it takes too much time and means they can't change their mind. They want to be in control, and secretly fear a plan might lead to other people holding them to account and challenging, or even criticising, their progress.

STANDOUT agency leaders are decision-makers. They're assured. They know what they want to achieve, and know they need help to achieve it. They translate their ideas into action. They make a plan and commit to it so that other people can help them turn their dreams into reality as quickly as possible. They fear that without a plan they will never have a clear direction.

Best-Laid Plans

Once you've mastered the first superpower, you're ready for the second. Having focus is one thing, but you must translate that concentration and commit it to a plan.

A few years ago, nobody would have dreamed of starting – or running – a business without a written business plan. Nowadays, it's far from being the first thing on people's minds. Indeed, in some quarters business planning is almost treated with contempt. The ability to be agile and to pivot have become more fashionable reference points. Some see having a business plan as too restrictive and a waste of time.

This attitude is not unique to digital agencies, but it's common. Digital agency owners find it difficult to plan. Most start out freelancing before building their agency. They're usually practitioners before they're business owners. Few have worked for any length of time in a big organisation. They have limited knowledge of how companies plan and manage their growth over a period of time.

Digital agency owners don't usually need to borrow much money when they start out. Unlike tech companies with large upfront costs, they don't need to pitch their business to investors. They don't need to convince other people of the viability of their ideas. A business plan can become an afterthought.

The work of digital agencies, particularly those involved in performance marketing, is focused on the short term. Tactical activity and immediate results are the currency for most. This, coupled with high client churn, means long-term planning seems futile for most digital agency owners, so they don't do it.

I feel short-term thinking and resistance to planning is a growing trend, not just in business but in the wider world. I've heard people start their reasons for not having a plan with the phrase: 'What if we had had a plan in 2019? Would it have included the events of 2020?' Clearly not, and I get the point, of course. We live in a fast-moving world and it's not going to slow down. Nevertheless, I remain an unashamed fan of making and using a plan.

Breaking Down to Speed Up

Many people dream of climbing Mount Everest. Those that actually do are not always the best climbers; they're the people who set themselves the goal, make a plan and follow it through. Nobody, even the best climbers, summit Everest in one go. It's a feat that is broken down into stages. Although each stage is hard, the overall task is made easier by the fact that it's split into smaller, more manageable, goals.

Sometimes, growing a digital agency can feel like climbing a mountain. It can be exciting, but it can also seem like a huge and daunting task. The best way to keep motivated, or in some cases even get started, when facing a challenge is to have a plan. Break down your goal into smaller objectives. If you have a plan of what you want to achieve it must include smaller intermediate milestones. Checkpoints that you can use to spur you on and measure your progress.

You may remember the exhilaration of hitting some small milestones when you first started your agency. Do you remember winning your first client? Recruiting your first employee? Breaking through that monthly billing target that had eluded you for a period of time? All these goals were, I'm sure, wildly celebrated at the time when they were achieved. They may now be long-forgotten, but it's important to remember the power of setting small goals and celebrating the achievement of milestones. They're a powerful tool in delivering growth and progression in your journey to becoming a STANDOUT agency.

Planning for Success

STANDOUT agencies know that having a plan is crucial to success. A plan will not stop clients making those last-minute change requests. Neither will it make those resourcing headaches disappear. It will bring something powerful to your business though. It will give you one thing that you must have if you are to achieve your potential. It will bring you control.

A plan is never going to predict global events, or avoid that unexpected client loss. But it will put you in charge of your own destiny. It will also encourage you to step away from the day-to-day demands of running your agency more often. No matter what challenges you face, you can always refer to your plan. Whether you are ahead or behind, you know where you are heading and what you are working to.

Nobody has a crystal ball, and the life of an agency owner will always be something of a rollercoaster ride. But having a business plan helps to flatten some of the big peaks and troughs. It can significantly reduce the anxiety of running an agency as you can always refer to your plan when things are getting tough. Unlike Adrian at Treadmill, STANDOUT agency owners recognise that rather than inhibit flexibility and reduce choice, a plan can actually give them more flexibility.

We're faced with so many options and choices both in our personal lives and in business. It can become overwhelming. Having a plan narrows your focus and commits you to action. It shows your team what is important and forces you to make decisions; to stop dreaming about all the things that might be possible and commit to making things happen.

For those of you thinking that a plan limits your ability to react or pivot, let me tell you that the opposite is true. Whatever objective you have, the route to it is unlikely to fall into place exactly as you expected. There will be many ups and downs. A friend of mine, Dr Jon Finn is a leadership expert with extensive experience in high performance sports and business mindset coaching. He knows that running a business or playing elite sports is never a smooth journey. During a conversation we were having a few years ago, Dr Finn summarised the importance of having a plan perfectly. He said 'Once you have a map, then you can start to explore.' If you have a plan with targets you know whether you are meeting them or not. It also gives you more flexibility, not less. A map allows you to make better, more informed, decisions. It gives you the ability to decide whether to take a detour from your intended path. It also gives you something to come back to if that pivot doesn't end in the way you expected.

Different Plans for Different Purposes

Whilst I'm a huge advocate of planning, I accept that producing long-term plans is not that useful. A plan doesn't have to be a forecast for the entire life of your agency. In Chapter 4 we looked at what vision you have for your business. What ultimately you want to achieve. Your business plan doesn't need to cover the whole journey to that goal. It only needs to embrace the next few years of your progress toward it.

What time frame should you work to when planning? When I was running my agency we used to work to a five-year horizon. These days, this feels a bit too far in the future to be spending time on now. For this reason, I work with my digital agency clients on a three-year plan. I find three years is a Goldilocks period – for those of you thinking three years sounds a long time, remember it's only 36 months or 12 quarters.

Now that you have a time frame, what should a plan look like? I still think there is a place for a written business plan. Whether you need it for financing or for some other reason, a written plan performs a valuable function. It forces you to think in detail. It encourages you to look at your agency not just in terms of the future performance but how it is performing now. How do your services and proposition stack up against the many other agencies out there? The very act of writing things down helps to clarify your thinking.

I use what I call a framework plan. This business plan doesn't require lots of words or detail, but it does include the key milestones to be achieved over the next three years. It's very simple and you can create it on a single page.

The Three-Year Framework Plan

My framework plan is built around what I call my Agency Operating System (AOS). The AOS is made up of seven pillars that form a framework to help you run your agency and plan its future growth and development.

The Agency Operating System

The seven pillars of the AOS are:

1. **PEOPLE** – All agencies rely on their talent, leadership and culture.

2. **PERFORMANCE** – You can't run a successful agency without strong financial controls and profitability.
3. **PROCESS** – Efficient ways of working improve how you operate your agency.
4. **POSITIONING AND STRATEGY** – Strategy forms the basis of any successful business model.
5. **PIPELINE** – Winning new clients is the lifeblood of agencies.
6. **PORTFOLIO** – Retaining and growing existing clients is key to building a sustainable agency.
7. **PRODUCTS AND SERVICES** – The range of services you offer and how you market them.

To create the plan, I first ask all my agency clients to think about where they are now across all seven pillars. What's good and what's bad? What are they happy with and what could be improved? I then get them thinking about where they want to be in three years' time. What does success look like to them in each of the seven pillars?

Some people find this planning process easier than others. The financial figures come easiest to most people, but don't limit your thinking to just what financial performance you want your agency to be achieving. What will those numbers mean for the number of people you need? Are you comfortable running a business of that size? What type of clients do you want to be working with? What services do you want to be offering (and do you want to be offering more or fewer)? What do you personally want to be doing? How different is that role from what you do now?

Once you have an idea of where you want to land in 3 years, it's important to translate this back into what that means for the next 12 to 24 months. Try and fill in some of the blanks. How many new clients do you need? What does recruitment look like? How much new business will you need to win to achieve your top-line revenue goals, etc?

Rather than a long, written document, you can plot the key milestones on a table similar to the one below.

	NOW	YEAR 1	YEAR 2	YEAR 3
PERFORMANCE (£)				
PROCESSES				
PEOPLE				
POSITIONING & STRATEGY				
PIPELINE				
PORTFOLIO				
PRODUCTS & SERVICES				

If you complete this exercise you should have the basic framework of a three-year plan. Now, simply print it out and file it in a desk drawer and come back to it later. No wait ... clearly that's not what you should be doing (as tempting as it is). Your plan needs to be brought to life. There is more work to do. You need to take the plan and focus on the short term.

- What goals do you need to achieve in the next 12 months in order to hit the milestones you have set yourself?
- What action now needs to be taken?

EXERCISE

Create a framework three-year plan for your agency using the approach outlined.

You can use a whiteboard, spreadsheet, Kanban board, or whatever you prefer to create your plan. As unsophisticated as it sounds, a stack of Post-it® notes and a blank wall are still my go-to option (particularly if you're doing this in a room with other people and you want to capture all the ideas and move things around easily).

Keeping the Plan Alive

Once you have a three-year framework plan, it should guide all your decision-making. The value of having something written down is immense. Psychology professor Dr Gail Matthews of Dominican University California led a study into the achievement of goals. It found we are 42 percent more likely to achieve our goals if we write them down.[11]

Whilst that's impressive, there's something even more powerful than setting a plan and writing it down – sharing your plan with others. The effectiveness of any plan is dramatically increased by sharing it with the wider business.

There may be aspects of your plan that you would prefer to keep confidential from the rest of the agency for the moment, but the more transparent you can be the better. If your team understands where you are heading and what numbers and milestones you want to hit, it's far easier for them to help you to achieve them. Once you have a plan, make sure you cascade it to the rest of the team. Schedule time to brief them regularly on your collective progress toward your goals. And remember to celebrate as many milestones as you can along the way.

---

11. www.dominican.edu/sites/default/files/2020-02/gailmatthews-harvard-goals-researchsummary.pdf

MY STORY – Year Beginning Meeting.

When I was running my agency, we tried to be as open and transparent with as much information as we could. Our reason for doing this was to engage the business. We believed that the more our people could see and understand the journey we were on the better. Having a plan is one thing, getting everybody on board with it is the next step.

Transparency of plans, goals and business performance is common now, but in the early 2000s it was unusual in private SME firms. We were early adopters of setting out our plans and communicating them to everybody in the business. This started with a company Town Hall meeting in January. We called it our Year Beginning Meeting (January was also the start of our financial year). We held this every year and supported it with monthly update meetings

Chapter Summary – THE POWER OF PLANNING

Planning is one of the three agency owner superpowers. In our fast-moving world you need to remain agile and more reactive than ever before. But far from being restrictive, STANDOUT agency owners know that having a plan can help them become more agile. They use it as the backbone of their business. They make quicker, more confident decisions, because they have a reference point.

A plan means they not only have long-term goals, but a series of milestones to measure their progress against along the way. Their teams have a far better understanding of the direction of their agency. They can see what needs to be done and appreciate what part they can play in making it happen.

Setting a target, having a plan and establishing team coherence is what gets you growing fast.

CHAPTER 13

THE POWER OF EXECUTION

Great execution is the ultimate differentiator.

Margaret Molloy, Chief Marketing Officer, Siegel+Gale

Life at a STANDSTILL

Adrian likes owning an agency, but he's not as keen on running one. He finds the operational aspects of Treadmill tedious. He's not interested in reviewing financial accounts, leading people or establishing systems and processes.

Deep down, Adrian is a practitioner. Doing the work is what he's always found most enjoyable. Running Treadmill has taken him away from his core skill set. He used to be able to manage all the delivery himself, but now he needs his team to help him. The problem is, he finds delegating difficult and managing people frustrating. He never quite feels like anyone can do something as good as he can. Adrian doesn't want to coach or train people; he wants people to deliver results.

Adrian's problem is that he soon gets bored. Once a project or initiative is underway he soon loses his initial passion for it. Because he struggles with management, he's constantly looking for different ways to approach it. He's always trying to deploy the latest management techniques.

Adrian is always looking for ways to revolutionise Treadmill, but he needs to understand that you don't create a STANDOUT agency by trying lots of different things and constantly changing your approach. You create it with the power of execution.

STANDSTILL agency leaders are changeable. They're restless and unpredictable. They love to start initiatives and do things differently. They get bored easily and are always looking for shortcuts and big leaps forward. They live for revolution and change. They think there's always a better way.

STANDOUT agency leaders are consistent. They're patient and predictable. They prefer to create momentum rather than chaos. They get a buzz from driving their agency forward by improving and optimising what they do. They live for evolution and optimisation. They think there's always way better.

STANDOUT Agencies are boring

Achieving focus helps you create a plan. But having both these things is useless without the third and final superpower. You must be able to *execute*.

You might find this surprising, but the best agency leaders are not always the most innovative people. Often they're steadier and more predictable. You may consider new ideas to be the driving force behind better agencies. Innovation is important, but the secret to being a STANDOUT agency is not to have a better strategy, but to have a strategy and execute it better.

A strategy is the foundation of any successful business, but even the most original strategy is useless if it doesn't get delivered. Execution beats conception. You must make things happen on a consistent basis. Boredom is your enemy here. In an industry that is ultra-competitive and filled with similar agencies offering similar things, as Margaret Molloy notes, 'Great execution is the ultimate differentiator'.

But what does being able to execute actually mean? Being a STANDOUT agency leader is not about having the best strategy, or the best ideas, it's about being able to put in the work, day after day. If you're not able to consistently put in the hard work, and are always looking for shortcuts and the next big idea, your agency will never reach STANDOUT status.

Developing a Routine

They say greatness is extremely mundane. Even the most successful people in business, sport or the music industry didn't get where they are out of pure luck. Natural talent often plays its part, but the greatest achievers in the world all have one thing in common: consistent hard work.

The key to execution is consistency. Consistent application of effort. Repetition of the same things over and over again. To be a STANDOUT agency leader you must get used to doing the boring stuff. Developing habits that work and sticking to them.

Our brains like routine because habits are efficient. When you automate common actions, you free up mental resources for other tasks. According to a 2009 study published in the European Journal of Social Psychology, it takes 66 days for a new behaviour to become automatic.[12]

Constantly changing your approach and looking to do things differently ruins the habit-forming process. It makes you less effective. It also makes it difficult for the people that work for you to follow you and your plans.

Consistency Builds Trust

To execute your plan you need an effective team to support you. Managing people is not everybody's forte, but you can learn and develop the skills over time. A simple but effective way of doing this is deploying a consistent approach in an authentic way.

Besides being effective at moving you toward your goals, a consistent approach brings other benefits. Consistency builds trust. If you are a consistent leader people trust you more. They can see what you are trying to do and know what to expect from you. They can understand what you want from them and what you expect them to deliver.

Having a clear plan is one thing, but to execute the plan you must develop a rhythm and a cadence of running the agency. Agencies are busy environments and are always extremely reactive to client demands. Bringing some order to the chaos by having a consistent approach is hugely

12. http://citeseerx.ist.psu.edu/viewdoc/download?doi=10.1.1.695.830&rep=rep1&type=pdf

beneficial. This means simple but effective policies, like having a set time for certain internal meetings and never deviating from them, setting a format for reporting, and establishing clear guidelines and processes for how things should be done.

What gets Measured gets Done

If you have a plan, it will stand little chance of being delivered if it is not accompanied by some measurable goals – a set of objectives to establish ownership and track progress against.

Everybody reading this will have worked with objective setting before in some way. Whether you prefer OKRs (Objective Key and Results), KPIs (Key Performance Indicators), KRAs (Key Results Areas), or some other form of measurement, the key is to make them SMART (Specific, Measurable, Attainable, Relevant and Time based).

I like to set objectives over three time periods:

1. **Three-year horizon** – What you want to achieve at the end of your three-year plan as explained in the previous chapter.
2. **Twelve months** – The objectives for this financial year (NB: Always work to your company's financial year not the calendar year). These should be in line with the three-year objectives.
3. **Quarterly** – Break down your twelve-month objectives into your goals for each quarter of the year. This will ensure you keep on track to meet your

twelve-month objectives and help you prioritise over the course of the year.

The process of objective setting could fill the pages of another book, so I won't cover too much here. My tips for effective objective setting are:

Keep them focused on change. Objectives are goals to aim for, but they must change your behaviour. If an objective feels like 'business as usual', it's not an objective. Your objective must specify what behaviour you are going to change. If, for example, you wanted to lose weight, your objective should not be: Lose two kg. This does nothing to change behaviour. It must be something more like: Go to the gym three times a week and order only three takeaways per month to lose two kg by the summer.

Keep them simple. Don't use elaborate language so that the objectives sound impressive. This only serves to increase the chances of people not being able to understand, misinterpret or remember what they're actually intended to convey.

Keep the numbers down. Have a maximum of seven objectives at any one time. Don't have too many things to focus on.

Keep the numbers in. Measurability is vital to progress and ultimate success. Ensure your objectives feature a number wherever possible. It's far easier to measure numbers than words.

Keep them transparent. There may be some parts of your objectives that you may want to keep confidential. Try to minimise these if you can. The more you can share the goals with your wider team, the easier they will be to achieve.

Keep them visible. When you have your objectives, make sure you and everybody in your team can see and easily reference them. Check your progress against them regularly. Feature them in the office if you can.

Keep them updated. When you have achieved or surpassed some of the objectives, make sure everybody knows. Update your progress and celebrate your success.

Optimising your Agency

Creating a STANDOUT agency is not always about taking giant leaps forward. The accumulation of small improvements can, over time, be a powerful way to grow your business. It can often be more sustainable too. Optimising and improving what you're doing is usually more effective than frequently changing it.

The power of small improvements is often referred to as marginal gains, or the 1% Rule. If you work on things that move your agency forward even by 1% every day, those small differences have a disproportionate impact. It's like the principle of compound interest and captures the essence and value of great execution. Small differences lead to big improvements over time.

Marginal gains is a concept famously deployed by Sir Dave Brailsford when he was the performance director of British Cycling. Sir Dave believes that if it is possible to make a 1% improvement in a whole host of areas, the cumulative gains will be significant. He has shined a spotlight into every corner of his cycling teams' operations. This has resulted in a whole host of small improvements. He has, for example, asked for the floors of his cycling trucks to be painted to show up dust. Specks of dust can get into the workings of the bikes. He demanded his team use antibacterial hand gel to reduce the possibility and spread of infections.

The 1% Rule states that over time the majority of the rewards will be achieved by the people that maintain a 1% advantage over their competition. In essence, you don't need to be twice as good to get twice the results; you need to be slightly better. In such a competitive environment as the agency sector, it's a reminder that you don't need to be completely different, just better than the others.

Using a Dashboard

The best way to deliver consistent execution is to consistently review your progress. The use of a dashboard to monitor key performance metrics is a great way of doing this. Dashboards are frequently talked about these days. Lots of software platforms exist to help us create and maintain them. APIs allow us to pull data from many sources. Tools like Google Data Studio enable information to be displayed in a clear and accessible way.

A word of warning here though, it's incredibly easy for dashboards to get out of control. What starts out as a simple summary of your agency's performance can soon become a mass of data as more and more metrics are added. I'm all for using technology, but I often see it taking over. A useful test is always to ask yourself: Would a simple spreadsheet suffice here?

There is also a tendency to keep reviewing and changing the metrics. Remember the key is consistency. My advice is to keep things simple. I recommend three or four core metrics across four key areas. I'm a fan of an acronym, so I call my dashboard my P.O.N.D.:

1. **People – HR and Culture**
    a. Happiness score.
    b. Churn rate.
    c. Training hours delivered.
4. **Operations – Finance and Process**
    a. Gross profit versus plan.
    b. Net margin versus plan.
    c. Chargeable utilisation rate/capacity indicator.
    d. Cash at bank.
5. **New Business – Marketing and Sales**
    a. Leads in the pipeline (broken down by lead source).
    b. Estimated value of the pipeline.
    c. Web traffic.
4. **Delivery – Clients and Services**
    a. Clients' Net Promoter Scores.
    b. Breakdown of revenue per service.
    c. Staff utilisation per service.
    d. Client attrition rate.

Balancing Board

One of the most valuable lessons I've learned during my career is to try to understand and appreciate the difference in people's personalities. Our ability to make plans, set goals and deliver them, depends on the type of person we are. Of course, new skills can be learned. We can all adapt our approach to suit different tasks and situations. But we are all naturally better suited to some aspects of running an agency than we are to others.

Whilst we are all unique, we do display some common personality traits. Some people are more outgoing, others are more reserved and reflective. Some of us are spontaneous and active whilst others are more stable and predictable. Some people are demanding and driven, others are more easy-going and deliberate.

None of these character traits are wrong or right, good or bad. Some approaches excel in some situations, others are more valuable when facing different challenges. What is important is that you have a balance of personalities in your firm. It's also vital that you have a balanced mix of qualities in your leadership team. Most important though is your own self-awareness. You must recognise what you are best suited to, and where you need support from others. Playing to your own strengths as a leader is a vital part of your agency's success.

MY STORY – Complementary skills.

During the 15 years my business partner and I ran our agency, we achieved great things. Whilst we both had similar goals and shared many common values, we were very different types of people. You could say we were almost polar opposites. This was evident to everybody, not least ourselves.

Everybody has their own strengths and weaknesses. In all walks of life, the best teams or partnerships are the ones that don't just compensate for each other's weaknesses, but who manage to achieve a balance where the collective is stronger than the individuals. They achieve a dualism where seemingly opposite skills and approaches complement each other.

Finding this balance is hard. It's not only difficult to achieve but difficult to maintain. Looking back, it's fair to say that my business partner and I had our fair share of ups and downs. I'm sure there were instances where we could have achieved better results more quickly if we hadn't been so juxtaposed. Reflecting on that period of my career though, I now see just what a potent force our complementary skills were.

If you can work with somebody who complements you, you can make progress faster and the results and experience can be so much more rewarding.

The business world is full of examples of great partnerships. Steve Jobs and Steve Wozniak, as well as Warren Buffet and Charlie Munger to name just a few. In their book, *Rocket Fuel*, Gino Wickman and Mark C. Winters explore the styles of two different types of entrepreneurs. They call them a Visionary and an Integrator. Visionaries are big-picture thinkers who like to solve problems and innovate. They can make great leaders, but they don't always make great managers. They can struggle to delegate, be reluctant to follow processes and they have short attention spans. Their alter egos, Integrators, are consistent and clear communicators. They're good at removing barriers and comfortable following plans. They like to hold people accountable to goals and objectives. Wickman and Winters note that it is rare for single individuals to be able to easily combine both approaches.[13]

Most of us have aptitude for one of the styles over the other. I don't like to pigeonhole people, but I do like this concept. Most agency owners I meet tend to lean more toward the Visionary profile. Nothing wrong in this, but it does mean that delivering plans is not necessarily their strength. If you consider yourself more of a Visionary leader, you need to have an Integrator to work with you if you want great execution. That could be a business partner, or a person you employ to work for you as a Chief Operating Officer (COO) or operations director.

---

13. *Rocket Fuel,* Wickman and Winters. Page 93.

EXERCISE

The first step to creating a balanced approach to leading your agency is to know and understand your own strengths and weaknesses. Personality profiles can be a useful reference point. Accurate profiling requires expertise and guidance, but there are many free versions available online to get you started.

Here's a couple to have a look at:

https://www.crystalknows.com/disc-personality-test

https://www.16personalities.com/free-personality-test

What did you learn about yourself?

Could you ask a business partner to complete the same test and compare notes?

Stepping Up a Gear

Despite having focus, a plan and a commitment to execute, sometimes you don't make the progress you want. Whatever your personality type, and regardless of whether you run your agency alone or with others, sometimes it still isn't enough.

It's easy to get distracted in a digital agency. It's understandable and very common. Priorities change and often the most important objectives get derailed. Growing your business can suffer due to the constant demands of existing clients. We've all been there. Sometimes you need something else to help you reach your goals.

Agencies thrive on two things: clients and deadlines. Running an agency is impossible without the former, and rarely does anything happen without the latter. You can use this to your advantage though. Find yourself an accountability partner.

An accountability partner acts as a pseudo-client and keeps you focused on achieving your own deadlines. Even if you're a process-driven type, you'll enjoy having somebody to support you in this way. Somebody you like, trust and respect, who can gently bully you into making sure you achieve your objectives.

Who this person is will depend on your own circumstances. Ideally, it should be somebody outside of the business. At the very least it *must* be somebody that isn't involved in day-to-day operations.

Friends can offer support, but a formal relationship is much more effective here. If you can find a non-exec, adviser, coach or mentor to perform this role for you it will work far better than asking a friend or colleague.

Objectivity is important to get the most out of this role. Even if you have to pay somebody, it's an investment for both yourself and your business. Moreover, if it's a commercial relationship, both parties demand more from each other.

MY STORY – Accountability partners.

We engaged a series of non-execs to help us run our agency better. We had a management team and employed a large number of people, but my business partner and I realised that we also needed outside input and somebody to hold us both to account.

It was very easy for one or both of us to offer each other excuses for not delivering on what we promised. We both knew the stresses each other had been under at various times. Whilst we challenged each other, we were both prone to accept excuses on occasion. We needed to preserve our relationship and we probably wanted similar treatment for our lack of delivery at times.

Our non-execs all had different styles. Some were more effective than others, but they all helped us to raise our game, brought us more accountability and improved our delivery on our objectives.

Helping agency owners to become more accountable and execute their plans is a crucial part of what we do at my consultancy, Beyond Noise. Of all the support we offer our clients it's the aspect that tends to be the real game-changer.

I've been told that working with Beyond Noise is like having an out of body experience(!) That may sound a bit far-fetched, but what they mean is that I become almost a representative of themselves. Rather than always put their own business behind the client work and down the priority list, our input enables them to put themselves as an agency firmly on the agenda. Issues are treated more seriously, more gets done and they make more progress as a result.

Chapter Summary – THE POWER OF EXECUTION

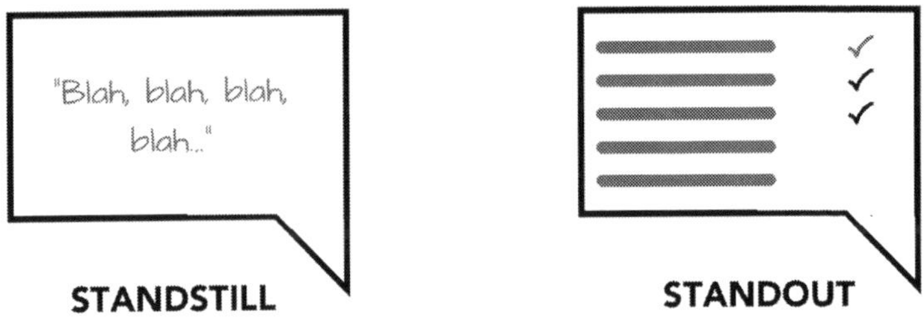

Execution is one of the three agency owner superpowers.

Generating lots of different ideas is easy. Putting some of those ideas into a plan is not difficult. STANDOUT agency owners know that execution and delivery is the hard part. This is what makes the difference.

Keeping focused on your plan, and engaging your team to deliver it, takes hard work and dedication. It also means consistent repetitive action. Something that your individual skills might not be best suited to.

Having somebody to work with you so you can bring both vision and execution to your business is key. Having somebody to keep you accountable and moving forward is a game-changer.

CHAPTER 14

THE END IS THE BEGINNING

Don't waste your time on jealousy; sometimes you're ahead, sometimes you're behind. The race is long, and in the end, it's only with yourself.

Mary Schmich, Pulitzer Prize winning journalist

Ask yourself ...

Thank you for reading this book. I hope you've taken something from it. As you've been turning the pages, my guess is that you've asked yourself three questions, probably on more than one occasion:

1. Is my business a STANDSTILL or a STANDOUT agency?
2. How will I know when I've achieved STANDOUT status?
3. Am I a STANDOUT leader?

The answers to these questions aren't straightforward and only you can answer them.

The fact that you picked up this book in the first place tells me you're not happy with your agency's progress. That doesn't mean you're *desperately* unhappy. Your agency may not be in a bad position. Indeed, you may be doing very well, but you want to achieve more.

Like our friend Adrian at Treadmill, your ambitions are not currently being fulfilled. You may have been running your business for only a short time and be desperate to accelerate your growth. Or you may have many years of experience and have just hit a sticking point. You're struggling to see where you need to go next. Many of you will be somewhere between.

STANDSTILL or STANDOUT?

If you're not happy, you're likely to be in STANDSTILL mode. Don't worry though. The fact that you've read this book tells me that you have bags of ambition. You recognise something is wrong and you're doing something about it. That's half the battle over. Armed with the STANDOUT agency R.O.A.D.M.A.P. and your energy and drive, you have all the tools you need to improve your business.

What's more, I'm sure there will already be some STANDOUT aspects of your agency. I've never worked with an agency that I didn't see something positive in what they were doing. I hope people learn from working with me, I always learn something from every agency owner I work with.

Being a STANDOUT agency means different things to different people. Some of you will want a small agency where you can enjoy collaborating with a close-knit group of people. You want to enjoy doing work for small clients where you feel you can make a difference. Others will want to open offices across the world and work with global brands.

The most important thing is that you're running a business you enjoy. One that is moving forward and not stagnating. Your goal is to own an agency that attracts the right type of clients; one that people want to work for. Crucially, you want an agency you feel proud of. We are all on a journey and each one is unique. So is every STANDOUT agency.

STANDOUT Status

There is only one person that can tell you whether you've reached STANDOUT status and it's certainly not me. Your happiness is the ultimate barometer, but you have three very important indicators. Your clients, your people and other agencies.

If you are retaining and gaining clients more easily. If your people are telling you what a great place to work your agency is and you have people keen – no desperate – to join you. And if your competitors are copying, commenting or even criticising what you're doing, chances are you're standing out.

What matters most though is that you are happy. The quote at the top of this chapter reminds me that our own happiness is ultimately what is important. We are not in a race with others but ourselves.

Some people are happy with six-figure agencies, others are desperate to break seven figures and beyond. How does your financial performance compare? What are you happy with? Whether you are only three years old and way beyond seven figures now, or ten years in and still a long way off, it's all relative. There will be people ahead of you and people behind you, whether it's financial performance, the clients you work with, peer recognition, or the effectiveness of the work you do. However, your goal is to achieve a level you are happy with and proud of. When you do, you will know that's when you can call yourself a STANDOUT agency.

STANDOUT Leadership

Whilst financial performance is important, it's not the most rewarding part of running an agency. Sometimes bigger numbers only serve to bring bigger problems. What I found the most rewarding thing about running an agency was the personal growth I and others achieved. Becoming a better manager and leader was the thing that I found most satisfying. Seeing my colleagues grow in experience, knowledge and confidence came a close second. Seeing how many of them progressed and forged fantastic careers for themselves was a close third.

Like the pursuit of becoming a STANDOUT agency, leadership is a journey not a destination. You will learn and improve over time as you become more experienced. But just when you think you have mastered leadership, you can make a mistake, or encounter a situation you wish you would have handled better. Making mistakes is inevitable. Learning from them is the true test of whether you are a STANDOUT leader.

Even if we become accomplished leaders, events outside our control can test our skills and experience in new and different ways. Anybody that navigated their agency through the COVID-19 pandemic can bear testament to that.

Your task is to continue to learn and grow. When you do, you must do your best to pass on your skills, knowledge and experience to members of your team. Help them to learn and grow and they will help you build your business.

Take Action

Regardless of how you measure your success, your journey to STANDOUT status is never finished. There is always work to do. Getting ahead of the competition is one thing, staying ahead is equally important.

The end of this book should be the beginning for you. I hope you have already started to put in place some of the ideas I've covered. If you haven't, you must start right away. There is no time like the present. The longer you leave it to take action, the more chance procrastination will set in, and the momentum will be lost. As I highlighted in the previous chapter, it's vital you harness the power of execution. If this book helps you to achieve marginal gains and improves your agency by even a small amount, I will be happy. I hope it delivers far more for you.

Enjoy the journey and experience of running and growing your agency.

If I can help you in any way I will. Please consider the following:

REVIEW

It's been a journey for me to write this book. I hope you've enjoyed it. I also hope you've learned something and taken something from it. If you did, please tell others.

I'd be grateful if you would leave a review on Amazon or via: www.beyond-noise.com/book-review

REGISTER

Register your ownership of this book at www.beyond-noise.com/standout-or-die and you'll get lifetime access to resources to help you on your journey. I will be adding new resources regularly and you will get updates via email when I do.

RELATE

You're very welcome to connect with me on LinkedIn at: www.linkedin.com/in/garethhealey/ Please mention that you've read the book in the connection request comments and tell me what you got out of it.

I'll also be delighted if you decide to follow me on Twitter at:
www.twitter.com/garethmhealey
Don't forget to DM me and tell me what you got out of the book.

REACT

If you have any questions, comments or feedback on this book, or about running agencies in general, email me at:
gareth.healey@beyond-noise.com
I promise to personally reply to everyone who gets in touch.

Alternatively, why not join me in a 30 minute online strategy session? We can discuss the book and how the principles apply specifically to your digital agency.

Book your FREE session at:
https://calendly.com/beyondnoise/standout-or-die

RESEARCH

If you want to see how your agency performs against others on the same journey, take the free online Agency Health Check at:
www.beyond-noise.com/agency-health-check.

It takes less than five minutes to complete and will highlight where your strengths and weaknesses are and what you need to prioritise.

ACKNOWLEDGEMENTS

First, I would like to thank you for buying and taking the time to read this book. I hope you've enjoyed it and taken some things from it that will help you grow your agency.

The book would not have been possible without the input of some STANDOUT people:

My wife, Laura, for her constant support and encouragement.

Sarah Houldcroft and the team at Goldcrest Books.

My awesome accountability group for their continued support and inspiration.

Daniel Priestley and Lucy McCarraher for their motivation and expertise.

Jake Mason, Mike Killen, Selina Bolton, Manpreet Singh and Chris Ashton for reading the manuscript and providing me with some great feedback and constructive criticism.

Peter Czapp for doing the same and agreeing to write the Foreword.

Finally, for all the people who I have had the pleasure to work for and with during my career so far. I have learned so many things from so many great people. There are too many to list, but I appreciate you all.

ABOUT THE AUTHOR

Gareth Healey

Gareth has over twenty-five years of experience in the marketing agency sector. He began his career in client services and in 1999 joined a Yorkshire design agency to head up their biggest account. A couple of years later he completed a management buyout and for the next 15 years ran the agency as CEO.

During his tenure, Gareth and his partners grew the agency into a £12.5 million, 175 person, integrated agency. Working with some of the biggest names in retail, they embraced the digital revolution, won awards for both their work and their investment in people, and survived several recessions. In 2014 they expanded their reach into London through the acquisition of a specialist digital agency.

In 2017, Gareth exited the business to focus on helping other people run and grow their agencies. He founded Beyond Noise, a specialist consultancy where he coaches and mentors ambitious agency owners. He enables them to realise their potential and achieve their dreams. Gareth has been a finalist for Mentor of the Year at the 2019 National Mentoring Awards, and is a visiting lecturer on digital marketing at Coventry University. He lives in Harrogate, North Yorkshire with his wife and teenage children.

Printed in Great Britain
by Amazon

75353370R00173